Daniel Simonovich, Robert LoBue (eds.)

Aspects of Behavioral Strategy

Daniel Simonovich, Robert LoBue (eds.)

ASPECTS OF BEHAVIORAL STRATEGY

Bibliografische Information der Deutschen Nationalbibliothek
Die Deutsche Nationalbibliothek verzeichnet diese Publikation in der Deutschen Nationalbibliografie; detaillierte bibliografische Daten sind im Internet über http://dnb.d-nb.de abrufbar.

Bibliographic information published by the Deutsche Nationalbibliothek
The Deutsche Nationalbibliothek lists this publication in the Deutsche Nationalbibliografie; detailed bibliographic data are available on the Internet at http://dnb.d-nb.de.

Cover picture: ID 298659315 © Skypixel | Dreamstime.com

ISBN (Print): 978-3-8382-1920-2
ISBN (E-Book [PDF]): 978-3-8382-7920-6
© *ibidem*-Verlag, Hannover • Stuttgart 2024
Alle Rechte vorbehalten

Das Werk einschließlich aller seiner Teile ist urheberrechtlich geschützt. Jede Verwertung außerhalb der engen Grenzen des Urheberrechtsgesetzes ist ohne Zustimmung des Verlages unzulässig und strafbar. Dies gilt insbesondere für Vervielfältigungen, Übersetzungen, Mikroverfilmungen und elektronische Speicherformen sowie die Einspeicherung und Verarbeitung in elektronischen Systemen.

All rights reserved. No part of this publication may be reproduced, stored in or introduced into a retrieval system, or transmitted, in any form, or by any means (electronic, mechanical, photocopying, recording or otherwise) without the prior written permission of the publisher. Any person who commits any unauthorized act in relation to this publication may be liable to criminal prosecution and civil claims for damages.

Printed in the EU

Table of Contents

Introduction 9

Part I: Foundations of Behavioral Strategy

Behavioral Theory of the Firm
Robert LoBue, Constanze Peters and Simona Rabuzin 13

1. Introduction 13
2. Outline of the behavioral theory of the firm 14
3. Overview of behavioral strategy 16
4. Impact of the behavioral theory of the firm on
   behavioral strategy 19
5. Research gaps and future implications in the field of behavioral
   strategy 21
6. Conclusion 22
References 22

Strategy and Cognition
*Ferdinand Fetscher, Chengyi Lin, Tamara Piek and
Daniel Simonovich* 27

1. Introduction 27
2. Shifting the boundaries of traditional strategic management 27
3. Cognition in strategic management 29
4. Relating cognition in strategy to the VUCA
   business environment 30
5. Conclusions and outlook 31
References 32

Strategic Decision-Making
Lisanne Heijne and Ziyed Radhouani 37

1. Introduction 37
2. Strategic decision-making and its relevance to
   behavioral strategy 38
3. Processes and models of strategic decision-making 41
4. Behavioral factors influencing strategic decision-making 46
5. Research gaps and future implications in the field of strategic
   decision-making 48

6. Conclusion 48
References 49

Organizational Learning
*Thomas Hellwig, Julia Hormuth, Michael Oberdorfer and
Christian Seifermann* *55*

1. Introduction 55
2. Learning 56
3. Organizational learning 57
4. Organizational learning capability 59
5. Conclusion and research recommendations 64
References 65

System Dynamics in Strategic Management
Robert LoBue, Margherita Pasquali and Oliver Vastag *71*

1. A brief history of strategic management 71
2. A brief history of system dynamics 72
3. System dynamics in strategic management 73
4. Reasons to apply system dynamics methodology to strategic
   management 74
5. Literature review methodology employed 76
6. The diffusion of system dynamics in the strategic management
   field 77
7. Organizational learning 79
8. Strategic planning 79
9. Performance management 80
10. Conclusion and outlook 80
References 82

Part II: Tools and Techniques in Strategy

Use of Tools in Strategy
Julius Nausch and Daniel Simonovich *91*

    1. Introduction 91
    2. Scholarly contributions to the field of tool usage in strategy 92
    3. Strategic tools and their practices 94
    4. Using tools in strategy 96
    5. Research gaps and future implications in the use of tools 98
    6. Conclusion 98
    References 99

Crafting and Evaluating Strategic Options
Senik Nikoyan and Daniel Simonovich *103*

    1. Introduction 103
    2. Crafting strategic options 104
    3. Evaluating strategies 105
    4. Responsibility for crafting and evaluation 107
    5. Research gap and future implications 108
    6. Conclusion 109
    References 109

Using 'Simple Rules' in Strategic Management
Madlon Peter and Deborah Chaya Simonovich *113*

    1. Introduction 113
    2. The idea for simplicity in strategic decision-making 114
    3. The simple rules concept 116
    4. Concluding thoughts 121
    References 121

Part III: Further Topics in Behavioral Strategy

Emotions in Strategy
Marcel Hermle, Robert LoBue, Yasmin Richwien and Daniel Simonovich *129*

    1. Introduction 129
    2. Emotions 130
    3. Emotions in strategy context 135
    4. Emotion in practical application 137
    5. Research gaps in terms of emotions in strategy 140
    6. Conclusion 141
    References 142

Neuroscience in Strategic Management
Karin Aviva Hirsch, Gerd Nufer, Robin Rüdesheim and Deborah Chaya Simonovich *149*

    1. Introduction 149
    2. The emergence and development of neuroscience 149
    3. Neurostrategy—limitations and criticism 150
    4. Neurostrategy—potential opportunities for contributions of neuroscience to strategic management 151
    5. Neurostrategy—research gaps and promising collaboration 152
    6. Conclusion 154
    References 154

Behavioral Game Theory
Robert LoBue, Jonas May, Jörg Naeve, and Lukas Schneider *159*

    1. Introduction 159
    2. Scholarly contributions to behavioral game theory 160
    3. Reflection on the state of research 166
    4. Research gaps and implications for further research 167
    5. Conclusion 168
    References 168

Introduction

In the dynamic world of modern business, strategy-making has witnessed profound shifts. Gone are the days when strategy was solely governed by stringent analytical models. Today, there's a burgeoning recognition of the role human behavior plays in shaping strategic choices and outcomes. "Aspects of Behavioral Strategy" is a testament to this evolution, offering readers an in-depth exploration of how behavioral insights are entwining with traditional strategic paradigms, reshaping them for the complexities of today's organizations.

This book is the collective brainchild of graduate students and alumni from ESB Business School of Reutlingen University, enriched by contributions from the school's faculty and from INSEAD. With this diverse set of authors, the content presents a blend of academic rigor and practical relevance, making it an invaluable resource for business students, scholars, practitioners, and anyone interested in the nexus between strategy and human behavior.

Part I: Foundations of Behavioral Strategy establishes the foundational pillars of behavioral strategy. Here, readers are introduced to the behavioral theory of the firm, unearthing the intersections of social psychology and cognitive frameworks with strategic practices. As we navigate the turbulence of VUCA (volatile, uncertain, complex, and ambiguous) environments, the significance of cognitive processes in strategic management becomes evident. This section further explores the realms of strategic decision-making, organizational learning, and system dynamics, laying the groundwork for this nascent discipline.

Venturing into **Part II: Tools and Techniques in Strategy**, the spotlight is cast on the continually evolving methods and approaches within strategy. This section invites readers to trace the evolutionary trajectory of strategic tools, grasp the intricacies of formulating and evaluating strategic choices, and familiarize themselves with the "simple rules" approach in strategy. The emphasis throughout is on strategic tools that are attuned to the imperatives of human behavior.

Part III: Further Topics in Behavioral Strategy immerses readers in specialized facets of behavioral strategy. This section dissects the interplay between emotions and strategic initiatives, highlighting the powerful emotional undertows that can either bolster or hinder strategy execution. Moreover, the promising confluence of neuroscience and strategic management is unveiled, suggesting intriguing avenues for future research. The section rounds off with a deep dive into behavioral game theory, underscoring its pivotal role in strategic decision-making scenarios.

In "Aspects of Behavioral Strategy," you are not just exploring strategy; you are embarking on a journey where strategic models intertwine with the complexities of the human psyche. We invite you to delve into these pages and enrich your understanding of strategic management in the contemporary business milieu.

Welcome to a world where strategy resonates with the human essence.

Daniel Simonovich
Robert LoBue

Part I:
Foundations of
Behavioral Strategy

Behavioral Theory of the Firm

Robert LoBue, Constanze Peters and Simona Rabuzin

Abstract. This article discusses the behavioral theory of firms and how it lays the foundation for behavioral strategy, which combines elements of social psychology and cognitive frameworks with strategic management principles and practices. The goal is to highlight key contributions from various authors by comparing their work. Emphasis is placed on the behavioral theory of firms and its significance to behavioral strategy that integrates social psychology and cognitive aspects with strategic management practices. However, this area of study is still relatively untapped, and more research is needed to develop comprehensive approaches.

Keywords: behavioral theory of the firm, behavioral strategy, behavioral research, organizational decision-making, bounded rationality, cognitive psychology

1. Introduction

Many publications in the fields of strategy and organizational theory have incorporated important concepts of the behavioral theory of the firm as a theoretical basis. Several authors have already addressed implications of the behavioral theory of the firm extensively, for example, in the fields of behavioral finance and behavioral economics (Barber, Heath & Odean, 2003; Nelson & Winter, 1982; Williamson, 1996). However, limited research has examined the importance of the behavioral theory of the firm for behavioral strategy and how this theory has influenced the overall field of strategy. Therefore, the article at hand examines central ideas of the behavioral theory of the firm and its impact on the general field of organizational dynamics, with a specific focus on behavioral strategy.

The examination begins with the following section, where the behavioral theory of the firm is defined and evaluated. Thereafter, the field of behavioral strategy is critically analyzed including its definition and different streams of research. Furthermore, on the basis of this analysis, the behavioral theory of the firm is linked to the topic of behavioral strategy, while the implications of the behavioral theory of the firm for behavioral strategy are examined in detail. Finally, research gaps are defined to identify further areas of study to potentially widen the field of attention in this topic.

2. Outline of the behavioral theory of the firm

A number of recent scholars, including Argote & Greve, 2007; Gavetti, Levinthal, & Ocasio, 2007; and Gavetti, Greve, Levinthal & Ocasio, 2012, emphasized the importance of the behavioral theory of the firm for organizational theory, as applied to general organizational phenomenon, as well as strategic management. In the following, a brief introduction to behavioral theory of the firm and its historical background is given.

2.1. Historical development of behavioral theory of the firm

According to Bāleanu (2007), the impetus for development of the behavioral theory of the firm stemmed from the seminal works of H. A. Simon in the middle of the past century, his book *Administrative Behavior* in 1947 and his article "A Behavioral Model of Rational Choice" in 1955. Gavetti and Levinthal (2004) stated further that many contemporary strategic implications of the theory are contingent on the follow-on books *Organizations* by March and Simon (1958) and *A Behavioral Theory of the Firm* by Cyert and March (1963). As a consequence, these contributions have set the cornerstone for the behavioral theory of the firm. These academic works are also often considered as having formed the early "Carnegie School conceptions", which were built on three assumptions: "organizations as the ultimate object of study, decision making as the privileged channel for studying organizations, and behavioral plausibility as a core principle underlying theory building" (Gavetti et al., 2007).

In general, the behavioral theory of the firm has a high significance for the overall field of behavioral and organizational theory (Augier, 2013; Augier & March, 2008; Argote & Greve, 2007). However, the behavioral theory of the firm did not only establish one single theory, but, until today, numerous behavioral and organizational theories, all treating different aspects of the firm, have been influenced by the concept of behavioral theory of the firm (Argote & Greve, 2007). Thus, by reason of its very open nature, the concept of the behavioral theory of the firm allows scholars to build on these multiple ideas of the behavioral and organizational theories and develop them further (Miner, 2015). It is hence considered to be a very broad-based theory (Argote & Greve, 2007). However, the core element of the theory has remained the same over the course of time, which is "a behaviorally grounded approach that treats bounded rationality, adaptive processes, and unresolvable goal conflict and ambiguity as foundational" (Gavetti, et al., 2012). In the following, a definition of the behavioral theory of the firm is presented.

2.2. Definition of the behavioral theory of the firm

While the behavioral theory of the firm is a very broad concept, consisting of multiple and varying aspects, its main premise was predominantly shaped by March and Cyert (1958) and has been employed by many different scholars over the subsequent years (Augier, 2013; Maslach, Liu, Madsen & Desai, 2015; Gavetti & Levinthal, 2004). Originally, the theory was developed as a critique of organizational theory and "viewed macro-level phenomena, such as price setting and resource allocation, as stemming from fundamental decision processes carried out by individuals within organizational entities" (Maslach et al., 2015). It remains a concept that "opens up the black box of the firm and accumulates theory and evidence on how a firm behaves as a result of lower-level processes, possibly involving individuals and groups, and certainly leading to observable decisions on economically important variables" (Gavetti et al., 2012).

The behavioral theory of the firm has been hence constructed on "organizational goals, a bounded rationality conception of expectations, an adaptive conception of rules and aspirations, and a set of ideas about how the interactions among these factors affect decisions in a firm" (Augier & Teece, 2009). Whereas the central idea behind the behavioral theory of the firm is, that a company is no longer viewed as a "mono-objective/mono-decision" entity, as it has been seen in traditional frameworks, but it is rather considered as a "multi-objective/multi-decision" entity where groups such as employees, suppliers, managers, customers, as well as shareholders comprise the entity of the firm (Bāleanu, 2007). Each of these groups possesses its individual demands and interests, consequently leading to conflicts, for example, regarding the allocation of a company's resources (Augier & March, 2008; Bāleanu, 2007).

An underlying concept of the behavioral theory of the firm has been the belief that decisions in a firm are intended to be rational but, due to human and organizational limitations, will never be completely rational. Therefore, a crucial assumption has also been that a firm consists of bounded rational individuals and groups (Simon, 1995; Cyert & March, 1963; Blume, Duffy & Franco, 2009) and that decision-making in firms is dependent on finding a satisfying solution rather than looking for the best possible solution (Cyert & March, 1963). While previous research into the workings of the decision-making process had confirmed and emphasized the importance of a standard procedure for recurring decisions (Allan, 1966), this implied that managing an organization involved handling bounded rationality in a developing business setting (Dew, Read, Sarasvathy & Wiltbank, 2008) and adapting its future strategies and objectives with regard to already gained experience (Augier & March, 2008). This suggested that organizations can learn new objectives, which contrasts with the prevailing opinion that organizations have unchanging values and strategies (Miner, 2015).

As seen in the above-mentioned analysis, the original works by Cyert and March (1963) and by March and Simon (1958) presented a particularly influential concept that still impacts scholars and the directions of their research. In particular, the fields of behavioral economics and behavioral finance have been strongly influenced by the behavioral theory of the firm. In behavioral finance, topics such as the investment behavior of groups vs. the investment behavior of individuals have been assessed (Barber et al., 2003). Fundamental economics concepts such as evolutionary economics and transaction cost economics have also been influenced by the behavioral theory of the firm (Nelson & Winter, 1982; Williamson, 1996). More recently, the topic of behavioral strategy has received increasing attention and has been discussed more frequently in academic literature. However, behavioral strategy has not yet been developed to the same extent as behavioral economics and behavioral finance. Hence, an overview of behavioral strategy is presented below and, afterwards, it is linked to the behavioral theory of the firm.

3. Overview of behavioral strategy

At this point, the term strategic management needs to be clarified since it is a fundamental component of understanding behavioral strategy. Early research was performed in the 1960s and 1970s where scholars such as Anshen and Guth (1973) and Meyer (1978) shaped the theoretical background of strategic management and established sub-topics, such as: strategy concept, evaluation, content, implementation, management process, board of directors and general management roles, and new ventures (Ronda-Pupo, 2015).

Indeed, along with the behavioral theory of the firm (Cyert & March, 1958), strategic management has been influenced by many different behavioral streams of research, such as behavioral decision research

(Kahneman & Lovallo, 1993), cognitive frameworks (Reger & Huff, 1993), and cognitive theory (Hodgkinson & Healey, 2008), as well as important values such as corporate attribution (Salancik & Meindl, 1984), emotions derived from intrinsic and extrinsic motivation (Nickerson & Zenger, 2008), attention of decision makers (Ocasio, 1997), and comparison of the aspiration level (Greve, 1996). However, strategic management in theory and practice has struggled to keep pace with behavioral movements in economics and finance. Strategic management theory lacks a proper psychological grounding, especially concerning the firm's heterogeneity of participants (Powell, Lovallo, & Fox, 2011). This point protrudes, because many firms suffer from poor executive judgement or from company cultures of poor and slow decision-making. Nag, Hambrick & Chen (2007) have also identified this lack of a solid foundation in psychology. Therefore, as was observed much earlier by Mintzberg, "strategic management has yet to gain sufficiently from cognitive psychology" (Ahlstrand & Lampel, 1998). Recent developments have emerged, which provide new opportunities for merging psychology with strategy, to fulfill an imperative where a dense foundation for behavioral strategy is based more specifically on cognitive psychology (Powell et al., 2011).

3.1. Definition of behavioral strategy

As noted earlier in this article, the term behavioral strategy does not arise often in literature and thus has no unanimously accepted definition. According to Powell et al. (2011), it is not possible to define boundaries, show methodological standards, give insights on the conceptual framework or have the chance to rely on supporting institutions, because "Behavioral strategy is a patchwork of theories and findings, and cognitive psychology has not captured the hearts and minds of strategy researchers." Yet, in order to fulfill a fundamental need for a common basis of understanding, these same authors did provide the following definition:

> "Behavioral strategy merges cognitive and social psychology with strategic management theory and practice. Behavioral strategy aims to bring realistic assumptions about human cognition, emotions, and social behavior to the strategic management of organizations and, thereby, to enrich strategy theory, empirical research, and real-world practice" (Powell et al., 2011).

To understand how this seemingly clear definition fits together with the premise of disunity of thought in the field of behavioral strategy, the authors present two assumptions that are essential. The first assumption consists of the identification of a lack of conceptual unity, meaning that the requirement for more psychology research is less critical, per se, than the integration of existing psychology understanding into strategic management theory. The aim is to bring strategic theory closer to the empirical facts and simultaneously embed strategic research into strategic practice.

The second assumption consists of the identification by Powell et al. (2011) that a foundation from psychology is lacking in behavioral strategy, meaning that behavioral strategy requires a theoretical basis from cognitive and social psychology. The authors further stated that it is important to allow for methodological diversity of research in order to provide sufficient evidence for the influence of individuals and of social behavior within firms or organizations. This encourages researchers to see behavioral strategy through slightly different lenses. For example, more recently, authors emphasized that behavioral strategy enables individuals to regroup after periods of separation (Montero & Gillam, 2015) or to have an effective influence on evaluative conditioning-based learning (Ludvik et al., 2015).

3.2. Influence on behavioral strategy by three schools of thought in the empirical domain

To a large degree, the diversity of research on behavioral strategy is due to diversity in the empirical domain. According to Tetlock (2000), the empirical domain consists of the reductionist, pluralist and contextualist schools of thought. The first school of thought holds that, "Reductionist research relies on positivist, realist, and objectivist philosophies of science and favors quantitative hypothesis testing using methods such as mathematical modeling, simulations, and laboratory decision experiments" (Powell et al., 2011). The reductionist school is mainly influenced by scholars who contributed behavioral psychology topics such as the overcoming of cognitive biases (Kahneman, Slovic & Tversky, 1982) and by authors that further developed the strategic decision process (Edwards, Weiss & Weiss, 2009), including a study showing that behavioral game theory is derived from assumptions of reductionist research (Camere, 2003).

The second school of thought as specifically described by Powell et al. (2011) holds that pluralist research builds on "multiple theoretical traditions ... entrenched in positivist, nominalist, pragmatist or evolutionary philosophies of science" and "uses methods ranging from case studies and simulations to large sample field research." The pluralist school focuses on the overall decision-making of the firm which is a result of bounded rationality, executive decision making in organizations, and group conflict (Powell et al., 2011).

The third school of thought holds that contextualist research encompasses the areas of management perception, the cognitive schema, the spoken language, and enacted environments. The contextualist school is embedded into constructivist, phenomenological philosophies of science and favors qualitative and interpretive methods such as textual analysis. In this area, the subjective beliefs or cognitive frames matter more than explicit decisions, which rarely comply with what firms actually do (Powell et al., 2011).

Powell et al. (2011) found, "diversity is the only reasonable option and that leveraging and integrating the three schools of thought need to become the first priority of behavioral strategy" and all the tools need to be applied in order to solve the research problems posed by behavioral strategy. This leads to examination of the impacts of the behavioral theory of the firm on behavioral strategy in the following section.

4. Impact of the behavioral theory of the firm on behavioral strategy

Reflecting on the impact of behavioral theory on behavioral strategy, Bromiley (2005) highlighted the potential of the behavioral theory of the firm, and thus cognitive approaches, to explain organizations' strategic behavior. This perspective is further supported by literature which followed in the strategy field (e.g. Gavetti et al., 2012; Argote & Greve, 2007; Augier & Teece, 2009).

The behavioral theory of the firm emphasizes the importance of the decision-making process to success and, in turn, reveals the difficulty of merging firm-level aims with the goals of all groups within a firm. Cyert and March's (1963) research into the cognitive foundations of decision-making in combination with the reductionist and contextualist school concepts provides a genuine foundation for a successful behavioral strategy (Gavetti et al., 2012). Freeman (1999) utilized the pluralistic school perspective to argue that behavioral theory could likely provide a theoretical base as a starting point of understanding behavioral strategy through linking aspects of psychology to organizational strategy.

Bromiley (2005) argued that even though the topic of behavioral strategy developed out of different streams of research, recent research topics form a foundation to describe a potential unifying framework of crucial aspects for this emerging field (Gavetti & Levinthal, 2004). In the following table, the main research streams of strategy, which are based on the behavioral theory of the firm, are highlighted.

Topics	Research streams in strategy that have a behavioral foundation
Population ecology - attempts to explain the structure of a company by considering births and deaths.	• Hanan & Freeman (1984) and Amburgey et al. (1993) highlighted the importance of routines at the workingplace • Hanan & Freeman (1977, 1984) observed that firms require acceptance from the public • Amburgey, Kelly & Barnett (1993) and Amburgey & Miner (1992) identified the cost imposed by change
Managerial cognition - fit of bounded rationally and cognition	• Schweiger, Sandberg & Rechner (1989) sought improvement in managerial decision-making by addressing conflict • Meindl, Stubbart & Porac (1996) and Sutcliffe & Huber (1998) showed that managers perceive certain situations subjectively rather than objectively • Barr (1998) and Barr, Stimpert & Huff (1992) indicated how strategic behavior is influenced by management's personal understanding
Top management teams - the structure and practice of top management teams	• Simons, Pelled & Smith (1999) indicated how conflict and performance are influenced by the group's dynamic • Rau (2001) showed how knowledge management of top management teams influences a firm's performance
Organizational decision-making - how firms make their decisions	• Eisenhardt (1989) and Bourgeois & Eisenhardt (1988) indicated how the quality of decisions is influenced by the structure of the decision-making process • McNamara & Bromiley (1997) assessed risky decisions • Greve (1998) examined how corporate decisions are made
Social networks research - information flow in firms	• Bell (1999) and Bell & Zaheer (2001) examined the different forms of networks and what information is shared on a network

Table: Research streams in strategy that are consistent with the behavioral theory of the firm (own representation based on Bromiley, 2005).

As demonstrated through the different scholars reviewed in previous sections above and by taking the different research streams of the table into account, it can be concluded that many aspects of the strategy field can be linked to underlying implications from the behavioral theory of the firm. However, it can also be expected that the field of strategy will continuously search for new, unifying approaches, that often build upon and include existing foundational concepts. With this in mind, Bromiley (2005) suggested that behavioral theory appears as a great opportunity, specifically that "The edifice is under construction." While Powell et al. (2011) pointed out that behavioral strategy builds on "past research in cognition, behavioral decision theory, organizational behavior, and strategy", but that this is just an early stage of research and many studies need to be conducted going forward. This is further supported by Durand, Grant & Madsen in their 2017 article "The expanding domain of strategic management research and the quest for integration" along with their citing of Mahoney & McGahan from 10 years earlier who recommended "the core agenda of the field of strategic management be extended" to include promising concepts, among others, such as social psychology and the behavioral theory of the firm.

5. Research gaps and future implications in the field of behavioral strategy

As shown in the preceding examination of the status of research, gaps in the understanding of behavioral strategy should be filled in order to fully define and reinforce its unique character and differentiate it from other accepted aspects of strategy. Based on the current status of scientific literature four questions are established that can provide a basis for further research:

- Is it possible to establish and define behavioral strategy as a unifying framework and, if so, what are its limitations?

- Which areas of research should be conducted and how can this be done to overcome the lack of psychological grounding of behavioral strategy?

- Can behavioral strategy rely on cognitive research already conducted in the field of the behavioral theory of the firm?

- How can already established ideas and information regarding the decision-making process as well as the best practices of the behavioral theory of the firm be transferred to the field of behavioral strategy?

Clearly, scholars have to marry the behavioral theory of the firm with the fairly new topic of behavioral strategy to attain new, profound insights and relevant conclusions for management practice. It should hence be helpful to fully establish behavioral strategy as a fundamental research stream in the field of strategy.

6. Conclusion

According to the review of the current and past literature, it is apparent that pioneers including Simon, Cyert and March were able to create a theoretical framework based on behavioral psychology, which offers a broad basis for an organization-centered behavioral approach (Gavetti et al., 2012). By reason of its very open nature, this approach permits additional scholars to build on its numerous behavioral concepts and further develop and elaborate upon them (Miner, 2015). Thus, these early authors were able to establish and contribute a highly respected and accepted concept, the behavioral theory of the firm, which remains relevant in today's business setting, influencing many behavioral research streams in business, management, and economics. The behavioral theory of the firm is therefore now a fully open concept consisting of many ideas that have been utilized by and influencers that have inspired many research streams in various directions, including, more recently, in the direction of behavioral strategy. Powell et al. (2011) have also more recently contributed a construct for the definition of the field of behavioral strategy. The behavioral theory of the firm in combination with behavioral strategy represents an emerging and promising field within organizational studies (Bromiley, 2005). Scholars agree that the development of the field of behavioral strategy calls for further research to seek a unifying approach, which could be achieved through the inclusion of already existing fundamental organization concepts, in particular, the behavioral theory of the firm.

References

Allan, H. T. (1966). An empirical test of choice and decision postulates in the Cyert-March behavioral theory of the firm. *Administrative Science Quarterly, 11*(3), 405-413.

Amburgey, T. L., Kelly, D., & Barnett, W. P. (1993). Resetting the clock: The dynamics of organizational change and failure. *Administrative Science Quarterly, 38*(1), 51-73.

Amburgey, T. L., & Miner, A. S. (1992). Strategic momentum: The effects of repetitive, positional, and contextual momentum on merger activity. *Strategic Management Journal, 13*(5), 335-48.

Anshen M., & Guth W. D. (1973). Strategies for research in policy formulation. *Journal of Business*, October, 499- 511.

Argote, L., & Greve, H.R. (2007). A Behavioral Theory of the Firm—40 years and counting: Introduction and impact. *Organization Science, 18*(3), 337–349.

Augier, M. (2013). The early evolution of the foundations for behavioral organization theory and strategy. *European Management Journal, 31*(1), 72-81.

Augier, M., & March, J. G. (2008). A retrospective look at A Behavioral Theory of the Firm. *Journal of Economic Behavior & Organization, 66*(1) 1–6. doi:10.1016/j.jebo.2008.01.005

Augier, M., & Teece, D., J. (2009). Dynamic capabilities and the role of managers in business strategy and economic performance. *Organization Science, 20*(2), 410–421.

Bāleanu, V. (2007). The economic basis in organisational behaviour—behavioural theory of the firm. *Annals of the University of Petroşani Economics, 7*, 729-736.

Barber B. M., Heath, C., & Odean T. (2003). Good reasons sell: reason-based choice among group and individual investors in the stock market. *Management Science 49*(12), 1636–1652.

Barr, P. (1998). Adapting to unfamiliar environmental events: A look at the evaluation of interpretation and its role in strategic change. *Organization Science, 9*(6), 644-669.

Barr, P., Stimpert J. L., & Huff, A. S. (1992). Cognitive change, strategic action, and organizational renewal. *Strategic Management Journal, 13*(S1), 15-36.

Bell, G. G. (1999). *The Influence of Geographic Location and Network Position on Innovation in the Canadian Mutual Fund Industry. PHD. Dissertation. University of Minnesota.*

Bell, G. G., & Zaheer, A. (2001). Instrumental but not enough: The influence of individual and organizational networks on communication flows. Paper presented at *The 2001 Academy of Management Meetings,* Washington, D.C.

Blume, A., Duffy, J., & Franco, A. M. (2009). Decentralized organizational learning: An experimental investigation. *American Economic Review, 99*(4), 1178–1205.

Bourgeois, L. J. III & Eisenhardt, K. M. (1988). Strategic decision processes in high velocity environments: Four cases in the microcomputer industry. *Management Science, 34*(7), 816-835.

Bromiley, P. (2005). The behavioral foundations of strategic management. *Theories of Strategic Management.* Malden, MA USA: Blackwell.

Camerer, C. (2003). *Behavioral game theory: experiments in strategic interaction.* Russell Sage Foundation; Princeton University Press.

Cyert, R. M., & March, J. G. (1963). *A Behavioral Theory of the Firm.* Englewood Cliffs, NJ USA: Prentice-Hall.

Dew, N., Read, S., Sarasvathy, S. D., & Wiltbank, R. (2008). Outlines of a behavioral theory of the entrepreneurial firm. *Journal of Economic Behavior & Organization, 66*(1) 37–59. doi:10.1016/j.jebo.2006.10.008

Durand R., Grant, R. M., & Madsen, T. L. (2017), The expanding domain of strategic management research and the quest for integration. *Strategic Management Journal, 38*(1), 4-16. https://doi.org/10.1002/smj.2607

Edwards, W., Weiss, J. W., & Weiss, D. J. (2009). *A Science of Decision Making: the Legacy of Ward Edwards.* Oxford University Press.

Eisenhardt, K. M. (1989). Making fast strategic decisions in high-velocity environments. *Academy of Management Journal, 32*(3), 543-576. doi:10.2307/256434

Freeman, J. (1999). Efficiency and rationality in organizations. *Administrative Science Quarterly, 44*(1), 163-175.

Gavetti, G., Greve, H., Levinthal, D., & Ocasio, W. (2012). The Behavioral Theory of the Firm: Assessment and Prospects. *The Academy of Management Annals, 6*(1), 1–40.

Gavetti, G., & Levinthal, D. (2004). The strategy field from the perspective of manage- ment science: Divergent strands and possible integration. *Management Science, 50*(10), 1309–1318.

Gavetti, G., Levinthal, D., & Ocasio, W. (2007). Neo-Carnegie: The Carnegie school's past, present, and reconstructing for the future. *Organization Science, 18*(3), 523 – 536.

Greve, H. R. (1996). Performance, aspirations and risky organizational change. *Academy of Management Proceedings, 1996*(1), 224–228. http://doi.org/10.5465/AMBPP.1996.4980460

Greve, H. R. (1998). Performance, aspirations and risky organizational change. *Administrative Science Quarterly, 43*(1), 58-86.

Hanan, M. T., & Freeman, J. (1977). The population ecology of organizations. *The American Journal of Sociology. 82*(5), 929-964.

Hanan, M. T., & Freeman, J. (1984). Structural inertia and organizational change. *American Sociological Review, 49*(2), 149-164.

Hodgkinson, G. P., & Healey, M. P. (2008). Cognition in organizations. *Annual Review of Psychology, 59*(1), 387–417. http://doi.org/10.1146/annurev.psych.59.103006.093612

Kahneman, D., & Lovallo, D. (1993). Timid choices and bold forecasts: A cognitive perspective on risk taking. *Management Science, 39*(1), 17–31. http://doi.org/10.1287/mnsc.39.1.17

Kahneman, D., Slovic, P., & Tversky, A. (Eds.). (1982). *Judgment under uncertainty: heuristics and biases*. Cambridge, UK: Cambridge University Press.

Levitt, B., & March, J. G. (1988). Organizational learning. *Annual Review of Sociology, 14*(1), 319-343.

Ludvik, D., Boschen, M. J., & Neumann, D. L. (2015). Effective behavioural strategies for reducing disgust in contamination-related OCD: A review. *Clinical Psychology Review, 42*, 116–129. http://doi.org/10.1016/j.cpr.2015.07.001

Mahoney, J. T. & McGahan, A. M. (2007). The field of strategic management within the evolving science of strategic management. *Strategic Organization, 5*(1), 79–99. https://doi.org/10.1177/1476127006074160

March, J. G., & Simon, H. A. (1958). *Organizations*. New York: John Wiley & Co.

Maslach, D., Liu, C., Madsen, P., & Desai, V. (2015). The robust beauty of "little ideas": The past and future of A Behavioral Theory of the Firm. *Journal of Management Inquiry, 24*(3) 318–320.

McNamara, G. & Bromiley, R. (1997). Decision-making in an organizational setting: cognitive and organizational influences on risk assessment in commercial bank lending. *Academy of Management Journal, 40*(5), 1063-1088.

Meindl, J. R., Stubbart, C. & Porac, J. F. (1996). *Cognition in and Between Organizations.* Thousand Oaks, CA: Sage.

Meyer MW. (1978). *Environment and Organizations.* San Francisco: Jossey-Bass Publishers.

Miner, A. (2015). The fecundity of authentic but incomplete designs and the future of the Behavioral Theory of the Firm. *Journal of Management Inquiry, 24*(3) 329–331.

Mintzberg, H., Ahlstrand, B. W., & Lampel, J. (1998). *Strategy safari: a guided tour through the wilds of strategic management.* New York: Free Press.

Montero, B. K., & Gillam, E. H. (2015). Behavioural strategies associated with using an ephemeral roosting resource in Spix's disc-winged bat. *Animal Behaviour, 108,* 81–89. http://doi.org/10.1016/j.anbehav.2015.07.014

Nelson, R. R., & Winter, S. G. (1982). *An evolutionary theory of economic change.* Cambridge, MA USA: Harvard University Press.

Nag, R., Hambrick, D. C., & Chen, M.-J. (2007). What is strategic management, really? Inductive derivation of a consensus definition of the field. *Strategic Management Journal, 28*(9), 935–955. http://doi.org/10.1002/smj.615

Nickerson, J. A., & Zenger, T. R. (2008). Envy, comparison costs, and the economic theory of the firm. *Strategic Management Journal, 29*(13), 1429–1449. http://doi.org/10.1002/smj.718

Ocasio, W. (1997). Towards an attention-based view of the firm. *Strategic Management Journal, 18,* 187–206.

Powell, T. C., Lovallo, D., & Fox, C. R. (2011). Behavioral strategy. *Strategic Management Journal, 32*(13), 1369–1386. http://doi.org/10.1002/smj.968

Rau, D. (2001). *Knowing Who Knows What: The Effect of Transactive Memory on the Expertise, Diversity-Decision Quality Relationship in Managerial Teams.* Ph.D. Dissertation, University of Minnesota, Carlson School of Management.

Reger, R. K., & Huff, A. S. (1993). Strategic groups: A cognitive perspective. *Strategic Management Journal, 14*(2), 103–123. http://doi.org/10.1002/smj.4250140203

Ronda-Pupo, G. A. (2015). Growth and consolidation of strategic management research: Insights for the future development of strategic management. *Academy of Strategic Management Journal, 14*(2), 155–169.

Salancik, G. R., & Meindl, J. R. (1984). Corporate attributions as strategic illusions of management control. *Administrative Science Quarterly, 29*(2), 238-254.

Schweiger, D. M., Sandberg, W. R., & Rechner, P. L. (1989). Experiential effects of dialectical inquiry, devil's advocacy, and consensus approaches to strategic decision making. *Academy of Management Journal, 32*(4), 745-772.

Simon, H. A. (1955). A behavioral model of rational choice. *The Quarterly Journal of Economics, 69*(1), 99-118.

Simon, H. A. (1947). *Administrative Behavior.* New York: Free Press.

Simons. T., Pelled, L. H., & Smith, K. A. (1999). Making use of difference: Diversity, debate, and decision comprehensiveness in top management teams. *Academy of Management Jourmal, 42*(6), 662-673.

Sutcliffe, K. M., &Huber, G. P. (1998). Firm and industry as determinants of executive perceptions of the environment. *Strategic Management Journal, 19*(2), 793-807.

Tetlock, P. E. (2000). Cognitive biases and organizational correctives: Do both disease and cure depend on the politics of the beholder? *Administrative Science Quarterly, 45*(2), 293-326. http://doi.org/10.2307/2667073

Williamson, O. E. (1996) Transition cost economics and the Carnegie connection, *Journal of Economic Behavior and Organization, 31*(2), 149–155.

Strategy and Cognition

Ferdinand Fetscher, Chengyi Lin, Tamara Piek and
Daniel Simonovich

Abstract. This article explores the evolution of research from classic strategic management to the inclusion of cognitive theory in strategic planning. Recognizing cognitive processes can minimize expensive missteps and can be intentionally leveraged in situations that test conventional strategic management, like in VUCA environments. However, more research is needed to validate these concepts, emphasizing the overall cognitive structure of organizations rather than just focusing on the cognition of individual managers.

Keywords: behavioral strategy, cognition theory, strategic management, cognitive management, VUCA

1. Introduction

In the past twenty years, cognitive theory has emerged as a key element in explaining results in strategic management research (Powell et al., 2011; Hodgkinson 2016). While cognitive psychology traditionally focused on individual mental processes, and strategic management on the organizational processes of businesses, there has been a shift. Concepts like intuition, creativity, and emotional intelligence have gained traction in strategic management literature (Sparrow, 1999), particularly as the field of behavioral strategy has developed. As described by Powell et al., 2011, p. 1371: "Behavioral strategy integrates cognitive and social psychology with strategic management theory and practice, aiming to infuse realistic assumptions about human cognition, emotions, and social behavior into the strategic oversight of organizations."

2. Shifting the boundaries of traditional strategic management

From its early days, strategic management prioritized logical and analytical methods, as highlighted by Hofer & Schendel in 1980. Andrews in 1980 mentioned that it encompasses purposeful operations, a focus on the future, and an adaptability to modify strategies based on results. Chandler in 1962 also pointed out its importance in deciding actions and allocating resources to achieve an organization's objectives. In common practice, managers gather and evaluate factual data, and then apply cognitive models to comprehend this data in relation to their operational setting, thus directing their strategic decisions, as noted by Daft & Weick in 1984. Yet, in situations with limited data, managers lean on heuristics to overcome cognitive restrictions, as observed by Kaplan in 2011. Analytical reasoning is paired with human discernment, which assesses data significance and decodes outcomes, as stated by Barnes in 1984. Managers also have the challenge of effectively communicating through the organization's internal channels to motivate and influence stakeholders during strategic transitions, as Sparrow articulated in 1999.

However, there are inherent risks with these cognitive aspects in strategy. First, there's the danger of managerial bias. If managers misread their surroundings, they might make detrimental decisions that negatively impact the organization. Second, there's the potential for employee detachment. When workers don't comprehend or have faith in a strategy, it can breed conflict and unrealized goals, a sentiment echoed by Barnes in 1984.

In the past, strategy heavily favored rational management, which underscores logical and unemotional decision-making. This standpoint took for granted that efficient, impartial managerial thinking was pivotal for organizational triumph, as discussed by Fineman in 1996 and Cooper in 1998. But newer insights recognize the emotional aspects of managerial roles. Although unregulated emotions can lead to workplace discontent, distrust, and anxiety, as highlighted by Sparrow in 1999, they can also spur enthusiasm and profound commitment. Sparrow in 1999 even proposed that managers' thought processes naturally turn more emotional in emotionally intense environments.

Thus, the realm of strategic management is in flux. Instead of just zeroing in on economic elements, it is now embracing aspects of human psychology, as mentioned by Hodgkinson in 2016. This is in line with a more general trend that values an organization's innate strengths, a perspective shared by Barney in 1991, complementing the customary external economic evaluations, as introduced by Porter in 1980. Contemporary strategic management recognizes the significance of varied cognitive abilities, intuition, inventiveness, and emotional acumen, as Sparrow discussed in 1999.

3. Cognition in strategic management

Managerial and organizational cognition refers to the range of individual and organizational phenomena associated with knowledge, beliefs, and intelligence (Laukkanen, 1994). People create mental constructs of their surroundings based on intricate processes that are influenced by existing knowledge, interests, and goals (Spender, 1998, p. 13).

When examining managerial cognition within strategic management, it is crucial to understand how pivotal managerial duties, like organizational decision-making, are executed and perceived. Kaplan (2011) suggests that the actual organizational structure plays a secondary role to the choices made by its managers. Emphasis has been placed on the significance of individual managerial cognition, the need to sidestep biases, and the prevention of decision-making errors in strategy research (Kahneman & Klein, 2010; Powell et al. 2011). To improve strategy outcomes, leading research recommends executives to enhance the psychological architecture of the decision-making environment (Thaler & Sunstein, 2009; Powell et al., 2011). Such psychological designs can positively influence employee motivation.

Next, we will delve into vital cognitive phenomena to deepen our understanding of strategy creation: knowledge structures, mental models, organizational memory, information overload, and cognitive biases.

3.1. Knowledge structures and mental models

Knowledge structures simplify information processing and decision-making for individuals, often based on past experiences (Walsh, 1995). Mental models, formed from these structures, serve as psychological depictions of situations, aiding individuals in contextualizing current perceptions (Jacobs & Heracleous, 2005). Organizations can harness the diverse mental models of various managers, fostering a 'cognitive community' to address multiple environmental perspectives. However, these diverse viewpoints can also cause internal conflicts, necessitating a balance between cognitive diversity and achieving consensus in strategic decisions (Sparrow, 1999). If managers cannot adapt their mental models quickly enough, they risk stagnation, leading to issues for both themselves and the organization.

3.2. The erosion of organizational memory

In recent decades, many organizations have outsourced non-core functions, often leading managers to lack firsthand knowledge in those areas.

The departure of experienced managers can also result in significant "corporate memory loss." To mitigate this, organizations should establish processes to ensure knowledge retention and transfer (Lahaie, 2005).

3.3. The dilemma of information overload

Information overload occurs when the volume or complexity of information becomes overwhelming (Weick, 1995, p. 87). Individuals may grapple with feelings of anxiety and inadequacy, leading them to fall back on familiar routines. For organizations, this can result in undue risk-taking, misprioritization, and inefficiencies. Thus, organizations need to strategize on shielding managers from such overload (Tushman & Nadler, 1978).

3.4. Cognitive biases in decision-making

Managers, being human, are susceptible to cognitive biases. These biases are consistent deviations from logical reasoning (Lovallo & Sibony, 2010) and often go unnoticed in decision-making processes. Biases can stem from ingrained habits, training, corporate culture, and even cognitive structures (Powell et al., 2011).

Heath et al. (1998) propose two approaches to counteract these biases: motivational repairs and cognitive repairs. Motivational repairs focus on boosting employee enthusiasm and can be supported by initiatives like creating autonomous teams or redesigning workspaces. Cognitive repairs, on the other hand, target the prevention of mental errors. Training managers to recognize and counteract their biases can be a powerful tool in improving the decision-making process.

4. Relating cognition in strategy to the VUCA business environment

The business landscape today is often described using the VUCA framework, which stands for volatility, uncertainty, complexity, and ambiguity. Understanding cognition can help navigate each aspect of this challenging environment.

4.1. Volatility and uncertainty

In a volatile or uncertain business climate, the ability for an organization to be flexible and agile is crucial. This might traditionally involve forecasting or preparing for a range of possible outcomes, often at a considerable cost. Cognitive theory encourages strategists and organizations to cultivate agile mentalities, capable of adapting rapidly to unexpected changes (Bennett & Lemoine, 2014). While conventional forecasting tools have their merits, they may fall short in highly volatile situations. In these instances, a strategy that combines both intuitive, agile thinking and deliberate analysis is essential (Kahneman, 2011).

4.2. Complexity

In highly complex situations, it is vital to prevent the "information-overload" syndrome in managers. Cognitive research supports the adoption of processes that tap into the collective intelligence of an organization's workforce without drowning them in excessive data (Sparrow, 1999, p. 145). Furthermore, targeted training can help individuals manage the stress associated with complexity. Without proper training, there's a risk of people defaulting to familiar but ineffective routines, potentially leading to disastrous outcomes (Sparrow, 1999, p. 145).

4.3. Ambiguity

Operating in ambiguous environments makes it challenging to make predictions and craft appropriate strategies. Here, Kahneman's dual-thinking approach – System I (fast) and System II (slow) – can be particularly beneficial. While System II's analytical and methodical thinking is suitable for structured planning, System I, which emphasizes intuition, pattern recognition, and holistic insights, is better suited for ambiguous contexts. Relying solely on data-driven strategies can be limiting in these situations. Instead, organizations should prioritize intuitive decision-making and experimental approaches, such as the minimum viable product concept. This method allows strategists to glean critical insights to tackle the inherent uncertainty of ambiguous environments.

5. Conclusions and outlook

Incorporating cognitive concepts into strategic management offers a promising avenue for businesses to thrive in the current commercial climate (Bennett & Lemoine, 2014). Yet, there remains a significant gap in research that needs bridging. A future direction for research might explore how these recommendations play out in real-world settings, given the current limited empirical data on their tangible success. Evidence from some leading organizations suggests that "strategists who can manage not just cognitive but also emotional processes are better poised to navigate shifting industry and market landscapes" (Hodgkinson, 2016, p. 1). Yet, as pointed out by Powell et al. (2011), an open question remains: Can a company's psychological framework, encompassing decision-making processes and choice architecture, be deliberately crafted to enhance executive decision-making? So far, research largely focuses on individual decision-makers, with limited insights on addressing organizations holistically when integrating cognitive principles into strategic management.

References

Andrews, K. R. (1971). New horizons in corporate strategy. *McKinsey Quarterly, 7*(3), pp. 34-43.

Andrews, K. R. (1980). *The Concept of Corporate Strategy (Revised ed.)*. New York, NY: Richard D. Irwin.

Barnes, J. H. (1984). Cognitive biases and their impact on strategic planning. *Strategic Management Journal, 5*(2), pp. 129-137.

Barney, J. (1991). Special theory forum the resource-based model of the firm: origins, implications, and prospects. *Journal of Management, 17*(1), pp. 97-98.

Barry, E. J., Kemerer, C. F., & Slaughter, S. A. (2006). Environmental volatility, development decisions and software volatility: a longitudinal analysis. *Management Science, 52*(3), pp. 448-464.

Bennett, N., & Lemoine, G. J. (2014). What a difference a word makes: Understanding threats to performance in a VUCA world. *Business Horizons, 57*(3), pp. 311-317.

Bennett, N., & Lemoine, G. J. (2014). What VUCA really means to you. *Harvard Business Review, 92*(1/2).

Chandler, A. D. (1962). *Strategy and Structure*. Cambridge, MA: MIT Press.

Chapman, L., & Chapman, J. (1969). Illusory correlation as an obstacle to the use of valid psychodiagnostic signs. *Journal of Abnormal Psychology, 74*(3), pp. 271-280.

Chermack, T. J. (2011). *Scenario Planning in Organizations: How to Create, Use, and Assess Scenarios*. San Francisco: Berrett-Koehler Publishers Inc.

Cooper, R. (1998). Sentimental Value. *People Management, 4*, pp. 48-50.

Daft, R. L., & Weick, K. E. (1984). Toward a model of organizations as interpretation systems. *The Academy of Management Review, 9*(2), pp. 284-295.

Doheny, M., Nagali, V., & Weig, F. (2012). Agile operations for volatile times. *McKinsey Quarterly*, (3/1), May, pp.126-131.

Evans, J., & Stanovich, K. (2013). Dual-Process Theories of Higher Cognition: Advancing the Debate. *Perspectives on Psychological Science, 8*(3), pp. 223–241.

Fineman, S. (1996). Emotion and organizing. In Clegg, S. R., & Hardy, C. (Eds.) *Studying Organization: Theory & Method (1999)*, Ch. 9, London: Sage Publications, pp. 289-310.

FMI's Center for Strategic Leadership. (2012). *Redefining Leadership: Strategic Thinking in Today's VUCA World*. Raleigh, NC.

Galambos, J. A., Abelson, R. P., & Black, J. B. (1986). *Knowledge Structures*. Hillsdale, NJ: Lawrence Erlbaum Associates.

Hart, S. (1986). Theory and measurement of human workload. In Zeidner, J., *Human Productivity Enhancement: Training and Human Factors in System Design (Vol. 1.)*, New York: Praeger, pp. 396-456.

Hodgkinson, G. (2016). Rethinking the psychological foundations of strategic management: Beyond cold cognition. *Research Seminar - Strategy & Entrepreneurship*. Rotterdam: Erasmus Research Institute of Management.

Hofer, W. C., & Schendel, D. (1980). *Strategy Formulation: Analytical Concepts*. St. Paul, MN: West Publishing.

Hollingworth, P. (2016). *The Light and Fast Organisation: A New Way of Dealing with Uncertainty*. Melbourne: John Wiley & Sons Australia Ltd.

Jacobs, C. D., & Heracleous, L. T. (2005). Answers for questions to come: Reflective dialogue as an enabler of strategic innovation. *Journal of Organizational Change Management, 18*(4), pp. 338-352.

Kahneman, D. (2011). *Thinking, Fast and Slow*. New York: Farrar, Straus and Giroux.

Kahneman, D., & Klein, G. (2010). Strategic decisions: When can you trust your gut? *McKinsey Quarterly, 13*, pp.1-10.

Kaplan, S. (2011). Research in cognition and strategy: Reflections on two decades of progress and a look to the future. *Journal of Management Studies, 48*(3), pp. 665-696.

Kinsinger, P., & Walch, K. (2012). Living and leading in a VUCA world. *Thunderbird, 9*. Retrieved May 15, 2016, from http://www.thunderbird.edu/article/living-and-leading-vuca-world.

Lahaie, D. (2005). The impact of corporate memory loss: What happens when a senior executive leaves? *Leadership in Health Services, 18*(3), pp. 35-48.

Langer, E. (1975). The illusion of control. *Journal of Personality and Social Psychology, 32*(2), pp. 311-328.

Langer, E., & Roth, J. (1975). Heads I win, tails it's chance: The illusion of control as a function of the sequence of outcomes in a purely chance task. *Journal of Personality and Social Psychology, 32*(6), pp. 951-955.

Laukkanen, M. (1994). Comparative cause mapping of organizational cognitions. In Meindl, J. R., Stubbart, C., & Porac, J. F. (Eds.), *Cognition Within and Between Organizations*, Ch. 1, Thousand Oaks, CA: Sage Publications, pp. 3-44.

Lawrence, K. (2013). Developing leaders in a VUCA environment. *UNC Executive Development*, 2013, Kenan-Flagler Business School, pp. 1-15.

Liechtenstein, S., & Slovic, P. (1971). Reversals of preference between bids and choices in gambling decisions. *Journal of Experimental Psychology, 89*(1), pp. 46-55.

Liechtenstein, S., & Slovic, P. (1973). Response-induced reversals of preference in gambling; an extended replication in Las Vegas. *Journal of Experimental Psychology, 101*(1), pp. 16-20.

Lovallo, D., & Sibony, O. (2010). The case for behavioral strategy. *McKinsey Quarterly, 2*(1), pp. 30-43.

March, J. G., & Simon, H. A. (1993). *Organizations (2nd ed.).* New York: Wiley.

Merrill, M. D. (2000). Knowledge objects and mental models. In Wiley, D. A. (Ed.), *The Instructional Use of Learning Objects.* Agency for Instructional Technology.

Montgomery, D. B., & Weinberg, C. B. (1973). Modeling marketing phenomena: a managerial perspective. *Journal of Contemporary Business, 2,* pp. 17 - 43.

Nisbett, R. E., & Ross, L. (1980). *Human Inference: Strategies and Shortcomings in Social Judgement.* Englewood Cliffs, NJ: Prentice-Hall.

Perlmutter, L., & Monty, R. (1977). The importance of perceived control: Fact or fantasy? *American Scientist, 65*(6), pp. 759-765.

Porter, M. E. (1980). *Competitive Strategy: Techniques for Analyzing Industries and Competitors.* New York: Free Press.

Powell, T. C., Lovallo, D., & Fox, C. R. (2011). Behavioral strategy. *Strategic Management Journal, 32*(13), pp. 1369-1386.

Sparrow, P. (1999). Strategy and cognition: Understanding the role of management knowledge structures, organizational memory and information overload. *Creativity and Innovation Management, 8*(2), pp. 140-148.

Spender, J.-C. (1998). The dynamics of individual and organizational knowledge. In Eden, C., & Spender, J.-C. (Eds.), *Managerial and Organizational Cognition: Theory, Methods and Research,* Ch. 2, London, UK: Sage Publications, pp. 13-39

Steiner, G. (1979). *Strategic Planning.* New York: Free Press.

Stubbart, C. I. (1989). Managerial cognition: A missing link in strategic management research. *Journal of Management Studies, 26*(4), pp. 325-347.

Thaler, R., & Sunstein, C. R. (2009). *Nudge: Improving Decisions About Health, Wealth, and Happiness (2nd ed.),* London: Penguin Books.

Tushman, M. L., & Nadler, D. A. (1978). Information processing as an integrating concept in organizational design. *Academy of Management Review, 3*(3), pp. 613-624.

Tversky, A., & Kahnemann, D. (1971). Belief in the law of small numbers. *Psychological Bulletin, 76*(2), pp. 105-110.

Tversky, A., & Kahnemann, D. (1973). Availability: A heuristic for judging frequency and probability. *Cognitive Psychology, 5*(2), pp. 207-232.

Walsh, J. P. (1995). Managerial and organizational cognition: Notes from a trip down memory lane. *Organization Science, 6*(3), pp. 280-321.

Weick, K. (1995). *Sensemaking in Organizations*. Thousand Oaks, CA: SAGE Publications.

Wrona, T., Ladwig, T., & Gunnesch, M. (2013). Socio-cognitive processes in strategy formation—A conceptual framework. *European Management Journal, 31*(6), pp. 697–705.

Strategic Decision-Making

Lisanne Heijne and Ziyed Radhouani

Abstract. Strategic decisions are foundational to the success and competitiveness of contemporary organizations. This article examines the evolution of strategic decision-making (SDM) theories, transitioning from traditional rational decision-making models to the bounded rationality approach, which acknowledges human limitations in decision processes. While various SDM models suggest structured methodologies, each brings its unique insights and applications to the table. Decision-makers are encouraged to embrace a comprehensive understanding of these diverse models. Such a multifaceted approach is essential for choosing the best strategy, vital for securing a competitive edge.

Keywords: strategic decision-making process, decision-making models, sequential strategy process, behavioral strategy, non-rational strategic decisions, rational strategic decisions

1. Introduction

Decision-making is a prevalent yet non-standard activity, riddled with uncertainties. Despite this, it is expected to align with an organization's mission (Papadakis et al., 1998; Shepherd & Rudd, 2014). Strategic managers regularly grapple with the disparity between existing challenges and available solutions. Such inconsistencies can breed frustration and erode managers' faith in their problem-solving tools (Bhushan & Rai, 2004).

Strategists, when at the crossroads of significant decisions, often neglect the sway of cognitive biases, opting instead for purely logical assessments. A revealing survey from McKinsey Quarterly, spanning 2,207 executives, found that only about 28 percent felt that strategic decisions in their firms were typically sound (Lovallo & Sibony, 2010). This signals a profound disconnect in managers' grasp of strategic decision-making (SDM). Identifying ways to refine the SDM framework and understanding potential roadblocks becomes imperative (Koklic & Via, 2011).

There are several established theoretical models detailing the SDM mechanisms within organizations. While this article traverses the vast landscape of these models, it also highlights the dearth of SDM-focused studies within behavioral strategy. The piece accentuates the nuances of

SDM processes, their defining traits, influential factors, and inherent limitations. It shines a spotlight on key thinkers who have contributed to both rational and intuitive SDM theories. The contrasting viewpoints of these scholars are analyzed and critiqued, drawing attention to existing research gaps.

2. Strategic decision-making and its relevance to behavioral strategy

Strategic decision-making has garnered the attention of many esteemed scholars over the years. Noteworthy names in this field include Mintzberg (1979), Fredrickson (1984), Eisenhardt (1989), and others extending to Bhushan & Rai (2004). Delving into the literature, several defining perspectives on SDM consistently emerge:

- Mintzberg (1979) views it as a definitive commitment, typically involving resource allocation.

- Combining the insights of Fredrickson (1984), Eisenhardt (1989), and Judge & Miller (1991), SDM appears as a dynamic ability where diverse managerial expertise converges to guide pivotal strategic directions of a firm.

- Eisenhardt & Zbaracki (1992) pinpoint it as those occasional, crucial decisions by an organization's top echelons that fundamentally influence its wellbeing and longevity.

- Schwenk (1995) describes it in terms of decisional rationality – the meticulous adherence to a structured process aiming for well-considered objectives.

- Bhushan & Rai (2004) encapsulate it as aligning internal competencies with the external landscape, opting for the most favorable alternative from available choices.

Strategic decisions are typified by their magnitude, irreversibility, and long-lasting implications. They serve as a nexus between predetermined and evolving strategies, often fostering organizational learning and personal growth across diverse corporate roles (Papadakis & Barwise, 1998). Differentiating between decision types, routine decisions facilitate daily business operations, while strategic decisions mold an organization's trajectory, earmarking resources, setting influential precedents, and steering collective endeavors (Bailey & Peck, 2013). Recognizing the gravity of SDM is paramount (Noorderhaven, 1995). This assertion is bolstered by research from Bowen and Bowen (2016) which posits that nearly all business choices lean more towards the strategic than the routine.

It should be noted that the definition and criteria of what constitutes a strategic decision remain subjects of ongoing debate in the field of strategic management. For instance, an article by Leiblein, Reuer, and Zenger (2018) entitled "What Makes a Decision Strategic?" delves into this very issue, emphasizing the complexities and nuances associated with distinguishing strategic decisions from others. Their exploration serves as an example of the broader discourse in the academic community about the true nature of strategic decisions.

2.1. Approaches to strategic decision-making

Earlier research delved into ethical decision-making within organizations (Ferrell & Gresham, 1985; Jones, 1991; Ford & Richardson, 1994). In contrast, more recent studies have shifted their focus towards the environmental and organizational factors that shape the SDM process (van der Horst, 2002; McKenzie et al., 2012; Gutierrez et al., 2015; Finedo & Olsen, 2015). A substantial body of work has explored the intersection between entrepreneurship and the impact of SDM on business performance (Smith et al., 1988; Busenitz & Barney, 1997; Busenitz, 1999; Lyon et al., 2000; Campos et al., 2015). Furthermore, numerous studies have dissected the decision-making process itself, offering insights into the intricacies of SDM (Schwenk, 1984; Dean et al., 1993; Dean et al., 1996; Oppermann & Chon, 1997; Elbanna, 2006).

A common sentiment among scholars is that the journey towards decision-making can be resource-intensive, both in terms of time and costs (Hoy & Tarter, 2010; Amit & Schoemaker, 1993). Many posit that engaging in the decision-making process necessitates optimism and a genuine commitment to participation (Connolly & James, 2006; Gigerenzer, 2000; Papenhausen, 2006). On the flip side, some researchers challenge this notion, portraying decision-making as a more neutral or even pessimistic endeavor (Busenitz & Barney, 1997; Flyvbjerg, 2008; Muren, 2012). It is universally acknowledged that decision-making is fundamental to all organizations. However, the strategies and methods employed by managers in this process can differ widely (Bowen & Bowen, 2016).

Noorderhaven (1995) highlighted four pivotal traits of strategic decisions: complexity, uncertainty, rationality, and control. Fredrickson

(1986) proposed that a problem's complexity directly affects the depth of an organization's SDM. Campbell (1988) elaborated on this by suggesting that the intricate interplay among factors that lead to decisions defines a decision's complexity. Uncertainty is another key player, with decision-makers often grappling with unknown outcomes arising from multiple choices. Platt and Huettel (2008) underscored the role of timely information, stating that its absence can amplify uncertainty, leading to information asymmetry that affects decision-making. March (1988) emphasized that the primary objective of integrating information in rational decision-making is to diminish such uncertainties when choosing between multiple alternatives. Bhushan and Rai (2004) synergized the ideas of complexity and uncertainty, noting that the challenges posed by both can impede the SDM process.

Rationality, as recognized by Noorderhaven (1995), becomes paramount when decision-makers, armed with sufficient resources and a deep understanding of the situation, aim to pinpoint the most valuable option (Bowen & Bowen, 2016). However, some researchers argue against an overreliance on rationality. Citing the inherent cognitive limits of humans, they suggest that decision-makers might not always be equipped to process all available information, advocating for more intuitive, non-rational decision-making approaches (Simon, 1960; Eisenhardt & Zbaracki, 1992; Conlisk, 1996; Williams, 2002).

Lastly, control is an indispensable component of decision-making. As Noorderhaven (1995) suggests, without control, decisions could merely become the passive result of various interacting forces instead of the active outcomes of deliberate choices. In a contrasting viewpoint, Simon (1979) proposed that once a suitable option is identified, it should be promptly embraced, culminating in a decisive action.

2.2. Behavioral issues in strategic decision-making

The connection between behavioral strategy and decision-making processes is an emerging area of interest in strategic management (Nagel, 2014). Recent studies aim to elucidate how individuals arrive at decisions, exploring both conscious and unconscious factors influencing these processes (Greve, 2013). Nagel (2014) highlighted that these unconscious elements can introduce cognitive biases. Interestingly, the nuances of decision-making haven't been explored in the context of specific strategic behaviors. A prevailing notion posits that humans typically make decisions rationally, aiming to optimize their benefits (Nagel, 2014). Powell et al.

(2011, p. 1369) defined behavioral strategy as the integration of cognitive and social psychology into strategic management practices. Essentially, organizational behaviors manifest from prior decisions. Thus, Greve (2013) recommends that businesses should first catalog these behaviors before delving into the intricacies of the decision-making processes.

Organizational leaders should be cognizant of several behavioral factors that play a role in decision-making. Grasping the objectives, processes, and influencing characteristics of strategic decision-making equips an organization to chart its path in achieving its objectives. Moreover, beyond simply choosing the most suitable action plan, it is vital to consider the nuances of execution.

3. Processes and models of strategic decision-making

A significant portion of the research on strategic decision-making focuses on its processes and underlying structures. Mintzberg et al. (1976, p. 245) describe the decision process as a series of actions and dynamic elements that commence with recognizing a need for action and culminate in a definitive commitment to that action. While there is not a universally accepted classification for decision-making process theories (Ahmed, 2014), one perspective classifies them based on the number of participants in the decision (Mintzberg, 1973). However, Brown (2005) suggests employing multiple SDM models. Over the decades, numerous scholars have introduced methodologies to streamline the vast body of literature concerning decision processes, including works by Simon (1947), Savage (1954), Cohen et al. (1972), Drucker (1973), Mintzberg (1976), March (1978), Wilson et al. (1986), Hart (1992), and Partovi (2007). A representation of a typical SDM method is illustrated in Figure 1, following.

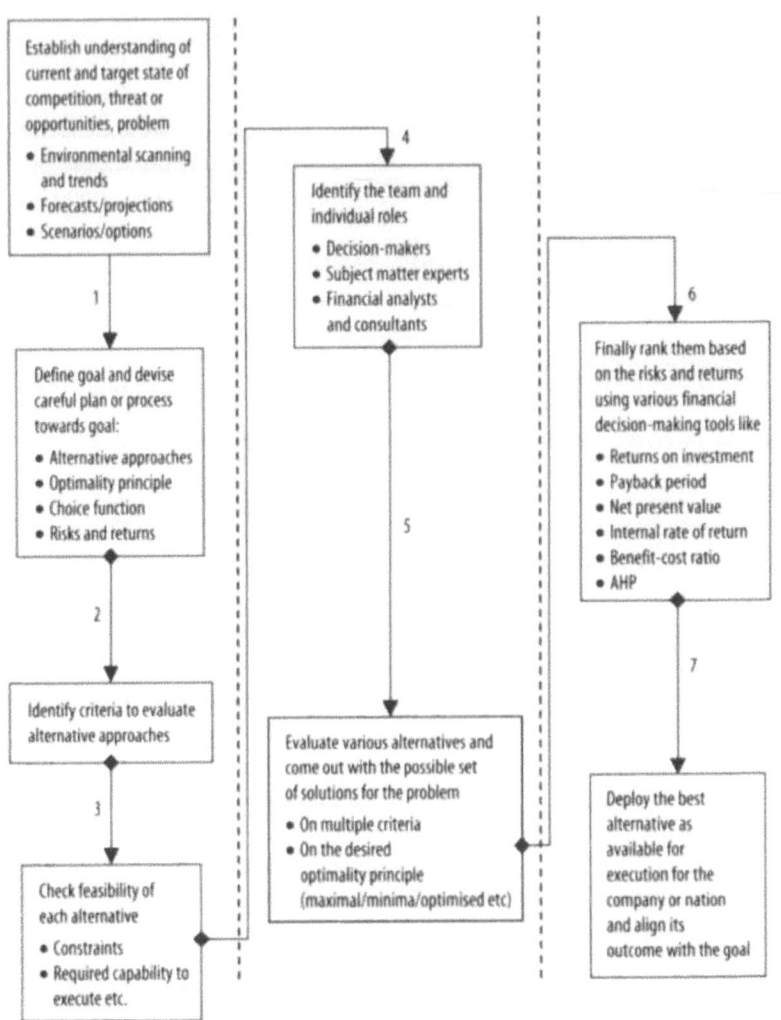

Figure 1: Strategic decision-making process (Bhushan & Rai, 2004, p. 4).

3.1. Rational vs. non-rational theories in the strategic decision-making process

Many scholars differentiate decision-making theories into two primary categories: rational and non-rational (Gigerenzer, 2001; Evardsson and Hansson, 2005; Oliveira, 2007). Rational theories typically exhibit characteristics like optimization, normativity, omniscience, and internal consistency (Simon, 1979). Nagel (2014) expanded on this perspective by showing that strategy is not merely about numbers, data, and facts. Instead, a behavioral strategy approach also delves into the brain's individual and social functions, as well as psychological and interpersonal processes, which transcend strict rational thought. This understanding aligns more with non-rational theories. Such theories are characterized by terms like non-optimization, descriptiveness, search methodologies, ecological rationality, cognitive foundations, emotions, imitation, and social norms (Ahmed, 2014). The distinctions between rational and non-rational models are summarized in Table 1.

	Rational/cerebral	Non-rational/insightful
Relationship between manager and managed	Control	Empowerment
View of organizational activity	Segmentation	Holism
View of the world	Totally rational: one best way	Limited rationality: multiple and perhaps competing rationalities

Table 1: Rational and non-rational models of management (Kydd, Crawford & Riches, 1997, p. 66).

In summary, Greve (2013) argued that behavioral strategies in decision-making vary in their degrees of rationality and influence organizational actions and results.

3.2. Theories of structure in the strategic decision-making process

Langley et al. (1995) highlighted Dewey's 1910 work as an early influential contribution to decision-making models. Dewey posited that decision-making consists of several phases culminating in a well-defined solution. Historically succeeding Dewey, Herbert Simon emerged as a pivotal figure in studying human decision-making behavior (Campitelli, 2010). Simon's 1947 work set a predominant trend in organizational theory by introducing a step-by-step decision-making model. This model, with its three primary stages, aimed to identify the most optimal resolution to a problem, as illustrated in Figure 2 (Levinthal, 2011; Paul et al., 2014).

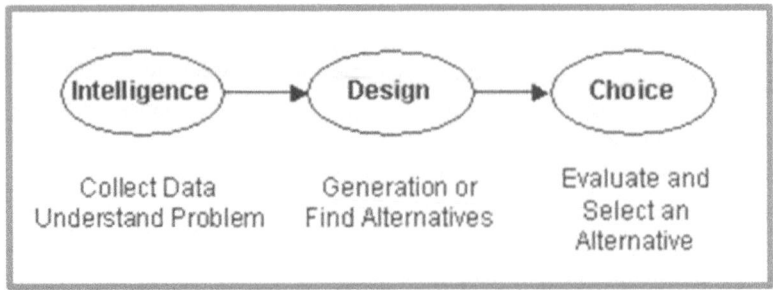

Figure 2: Simon's sequential decision-making model (adapted from Paul et al., 2014).

Simon (1949) introduced the idea that individuals often "satisfice" when making decisions, rather than seeking to maximize their choice. He posited that, due to the human brain's cognitive constraints and the intricate nature of real-world situations, attaining true maximization is nearly unfeasible. In essence, decision-makers often opt for an option that meets a basic adequacy criterion—the first solution they encounter that's satisfactory—instead of exhaustively analyzing all potential alternatives for their associated costs and benefits. Hence, to "satisfice" means settling for a choice that is adequate, rather than pursuing the absolute best (Campitelli, 2010).

However, Simon's model has not been universally embraced. Various scholars have critiqued it, noting that the model delves into diverse psychological domains like perception, imagery, cognition, and memory, rather than focusing squarely on decision-making (Campitelli & Gobet, 2010). Schwenk (1985) argued that the model might embed inherent biases, leading individuals to mistakenly perceive certain options as more logical than they truly are. Moreover, Simon's step-by-step approach has faced skepticism, particularly in situations involving multiple decision-makers, ambiguous organizational objectives, and dispersed corporate actions (Weiss, 1982; Allison, 1999).

Yet, Simon's perspective has greatly influenced subsequent academic work in the realm of organizational decision-making. His contributions gained further prominence following his Nobel Prize in economics (Leahey, 2003). Building on Simon's foundation, Mintzberg et al. (1976) proposed their "general model of the strategic decision-making process," suggesting that even though strategic decisions can be profoundly intricate and dynamic, a coherent conceptual framework can still delineate the process, as depicted in Figure 3.

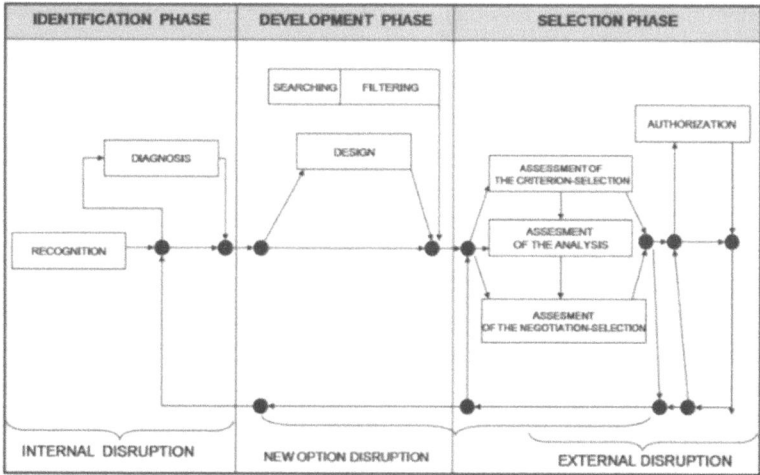

Figure 3: Applying process structure to unstructured SDM (adapted from Mintzberg et al., 1976, p. 266.),

As also incorporated in Figure 3, researchers identified three core stages in the strategic decision-making process: identification, development, and selection. To transition from one phase to the next, particular routines must be met, and myriad dynamic factors can sway the final decision.

Subsequent research has aimed to categorize the various SDM processes. Hicksen et al. (1986) identified three fundamental types of processes—fluid, constricted, and sporadic—each defined by its characteristics. Fluid processes progress steadily; constricted processes limit effort in gathering information and participant involvement; while sporadic processes experience interruptions and might revisit several steps before finalizing a decision (Wilson et al., 1986).

The Garbage Can model from Cohen et al. (1972) posits the SDM process as a confluence of actors, goals, and perspectives. March (1978) emphasizes that decision-making in organizations is not isolated but intertwined with established procedures, group dialogues, and politics. However, Das and Teng (1999) warn that an excessive focus on organizational processes might stifle innovative thinking.

Hitt and Tyler (1991) found most companies (over 80%) lean towards rationality in the SDM process, aligning with the belief that decisions should be made without bias (Mintzberg et al., 1976). Fredrickson

(1984) suggests decision-making is both rational and intuitive, a notion expanded by Citroen who, synthesizing works from Drucker (1967), Mintzberg et al. (1976), and others, formulated a seven-step structured decision-making process. Essentially, it involves identifying problems, seeking alternatives, weighing pros and cons, being open to new information, re-evaluating alternatives, preparing for implementation, and setting up a review mechanism.

In their view, making rational decisions requires grasping the ramifications of all potential choices. Mintzberg et al. (1976) articulate this by suggesting decision-makers transform unstructured problems into structured components.

Hart (1992) offers an integrative framework incorporating various strategy-making styles. However, Simon (1979) counters that real-world application is not so straightforward, given unpredictable external factors and human cognitive limitations. Savage's (1954) theory touches on decision-making amidst risk, but Elster (1983) points out that sometimes there's insufficient data to gauge potential risks, complicating SDM.

In decision-making, information search is crucial, but while some rational theories assume all information is readily accessible, others, like "optimization under constraints", acknowledge search limitations but aim for optimization (Dantzig, 1955; Charnes & Cooper, 1963). These theories have been criticized for overly focusing on the cost-benefit of the search rather than on the strategic choices themselves (Gigerenzer, 2001).

Overall, while many agree that the decision-making process encompasses distinct stages, there's contention over whether these stages necessarily signify a structured, information-driven process evaluating multiple alternatives.

4. Behavioral factors influencing strategic decision-making

Various behavioral factors can impact decision-making, sometimes negatively. Such factors include the escalation of commitment (Staw, 1976; Mahring & Keil, 2008), the sunk cost effect (Arkes & Blumer, 1985), and optimization under constraints theories (Dantzig 1955; Charnes & Cooper, 1963). These behavioral influences led to the development of models such as image theory (Beach, 1990) and prospect theory (Kahneman & Tversky, 1979) to address cognitive biases that shape the heuristics individuals use when making decisions (Mitchell, Dean, & Sharfman, 2011). The presence of influential colleagues, for instance, might sway a decision-maker to favor a specific choice (Busenitz & Barney, 1997), pointing to the unpredictability of decision-making and the importance of considering biases in the strategic decision-making process.

Zajonc (1980) spotlighted emotional affect as a potential bias in decision-making. Dual-process theories further elaborate on this, noting that personal experiences are automatically factored into decisions with an emotional bias (Epstein, 1994). Additionally, heuristic affect is relevant in decision-making, as it suggests that individuals often approximate solutions rather than delve deep into analysis (Slovic et al., 2002). The surrounding environment has a role in SDM (Hutzschenreuter & Kleindienst, 2006; Dean & Sharfman, 1996), and individual variations in SDM can often trace back to a decision-maker's own history (Forbes, 2005; Judge & Miller, 1991). Another factor to consider is the metacognitive experience, which can sometimes lead to unpredictable strategic choices (Mitchell, Dean, & Sharfman, 2011). Schwenk (1988) compiled a list, shown in Table 2, of heuristics and biases most likely to influence SDM.

Bias	Effects
(1) Availability	(1) Judgements of probability of easily-recalled events distorted.
(2) Selective perception	(2) Expectations may bias observations of variables relevant to strategy.
(3) Illusory correlation	(3) Encourages belief that unrelated variables are correlated.
(4) Conservatism	(4) Failure sufficiently to revise forecasts based on new information.
(5) Law of *small* numbers	(5) Overestimation of the degree to which small samples are representative of populations.
(6) Regression bias	(6) Failure to allow for regression to the mean.
(7) Wishful thinking	(7) Probability of desired outcomes judged to be inappropriately high.
(8) Illusion of control	(8) Overestimation of personal control over outcomes.
(9) Logical reconstruction	(9) 'Logical' reconstruction of events which cannot be accurately recalled.
(10) Hindsight bias	(10) Overestimation of predictability of past events.

Table 2: Selected heuristics and biases in SDM (Schwenk, 1988, p. 44).

Thus, research indicates the importance of recognizing and addressing numerous behavioral factors in strategic decision-making to prevent incorrect decisions stemming from inherent biases.

5. Research gaps and future implications in the field of strategic decision-making

Despite the extensive body of work on strategic decision-making, there remain several areas where research is notably sparse (Lo & Lys, 2000). One of the significant gaps is the limited exploration of SDM in an expansive international context. Additionally, while numerous SDM models have been introduced, they often lack sufficient detail and overwhelmingly favor rational theory. It is also concerning that, even though SDM is inherently multifaceted, studies typically narrow their scope to single attributes, such as comprehensiveness or decentralization. However, a silver lining emerges with the assertion of Powell et al. (2011) that behavioral economics and finance have been trailblazers in merging disciplines, pointing towards potential intersections with psychology and neuroscience. These intersections present an exciting avenue for future research, which might pave the way for the development of innovative SDM models that cater to diverse organizational needs.

6. Conclusion

Strategic decisions are paramount to the vitality of contemporary organizations. To maximize effectiveness in strategy development and implementation, it is imperative to select an SDM process that resonates with an organization's core values and aspirations. This discussion has spanned a spectrum of viewpoints on SDM theory, revealing the interplay and potential influence of affect, individual differences, biases, and external environments on SDM alternatives.

Historically, models of rational decision-making held sway, emphasizing a clear, logic-driven approach to choosing between alternatives. However, a shift occurred with the introduction of the bounded rationality approach, such as Simon's model, which factored in the limitations and imperfections inherent in human decision-making. This approach has significantly shaped strategy research in recent times. Interestingly, as technology advances, especially in the realm of data analytics, there is a noticeable trend returning to more rational decision-making models. The capabilities offered by modern analytics, as highlighted by works such as "Prediction Machines" by Agrawal, Gans, and Goldfarb (2018), are filling information gaps and refining prediction methodologies, prompting a reevaluation of purely bounded rationality models.

While various SDM models advocate for a structured process—complete with sequences of phases or steps—their distinct methodologies and foundations offer diverse insights and applications. These models, each with its unique merits, illuminate SDM from various angles, enriching the theoretical dialogue. As the world of strategic decision-making oscillates between time-tested models and the allure of data-driven methodologies, decision-makers are urged to approach their strategies with a composite understanding, which includes behavioral aspects. Otherwise, they might miss out on critical opportunities to select the best strategic alternative, crucial for securing a competitive advantage.

References

Agrawal, A., Gans, J., & Goldfarb, A. (2018). *Predicton Machines: The Simple Economics of Artificial Intelligence.* Campridge, MA, USA: Harvard Business Press.

Ahmed, A. B. (2014). Strategic decision making: Process, models, and theories. *Business Management and Strategy, 5*(1), 78-104.

Allison, G., & Zelikow, P. (1999). *Essence of decision: Explaining the Cuban missile crisis.* New York: Longman.

Amit, R., & Shoemaker, P. (1993). Strategic assets and organizational rent. *Strategic Management Journal, 14*(1), 33-46.

Arkes, H., & Blumer, C. (1985). The psychology of sunk cost. *Organizational Behaviour and Human Decision Processes, 35,* 124-140.

Atkinson, P. E. (2012). Return on investment in executive coaching: effective organisational change. *Management Services, Spring,* 20-23.

Bailey, B. C., & Peck, S. I. (2013). Boardroom strategic decision-making style: Understanding the antecedents. *Corporate Governance: An International Review, 21*(2), 131-146.

Beach, L. (1990). *Image Theory: Decision Making in Personal and Organizational Contexts.* Chichester: Wiley.

Bhushan, N., & Rai, K. (2004). *Strategic Decision Making: Applying the Analytic Hierarchy Process.* London: Springer.

Bowen, G., & Bowen, D. (2016). Social media: A strategic decision making tool. *Journal of Global Business and Technology,* 48-59.

Brown, W. A. (2005). Exploring the association between board and organizational performance in nonprofit organizations. *Nonprofit Management and Leadership, 15*(3), 317-339.

Busenitz, L. (1999). Entrepreneurial risk and strategic decision making: It's a matter of perspective. *The Journal of Applied Behavioral Science, September,* 325-340.

Busenitz, L., & Barney, J. (1997). Differences between entrepreneurs and managers in large organizations: Biases and heuristics in strategic decision-making. *Journal of Business Venturing, 12*(1), 9-30.

Campbell, D. (1988). Task complexity: A review and analysis. *Academy of Management Review, 13*(1), 40-52.

Campitelli, G. &. (2010). Herbert Simon's decision-making approach: Investigation of cognitive processes in experts. *General Psychology, 14*(4), 354.

Campos, H., Parellada, F., Atondo, G., & Quintero, M. (2015). Strategic decision making, entrpreneurial orientation and performance: An organizational life cycle approach. *Revista De Administração FACES Journal*, 9-24.

Charnes, A., & Cooper, W. (1963). Deterministic equivalents for optimizing and satisficing under chance constraints. *Operations Research, 11*(1), 18-39.

Citroen, C. L. (2011). The role of information in strategic decision-making. *International Journa of Information Management, 31*, 493-501.

Cohen, M., March, J., & Olsen, J. (1972). A garbage can model of organizational choice. *Administrative Science Quarterly*, 1-25.

Connolly, M., & James, C. (2006). Collaboration for school improvement: A resource dependency and institutional framework of analysis. *Educational Management Administration & Leadership, 34*(1), 69-87.

Dantzig, G. B. (1955). Linear programming under uncertainty. *Management Science, 1*(3-4), 197-206.

Das, T., & Teng, B. (1999). Cognitive biases and strategic decision processes: An integrative perspective. *Journal of Management Studies, 36*(6), 757-778.

Dean, J., & Sharfman, M. (1993). Procedural rationality in the strategic decision-making process. *Journal of Management Studies, 30*(4), 587-610.

Dean, J., & Sharfman, M. (1996). Does decision process matter? A study of strategic decision-making effectiveness. *Academy of Management Journal, 39*(2), 368-392.

Drucker, P. (1973). *Management: Tasks, Responsibilities, Practices*. New York: Harper & Row.

Drucker, P. F. (1967). *The Effective Decision*. Harvard University. Graduate School of Business Administration.

Edvardsson, K., & Hansson, S. O. (2005). When is a goal rational?. *Social Choice and Welfare, 24*(2), 343-361.

Eisenhardt, K. (1989). Agency Theory: An assessment and review. . *Academy of Management Review, 14*(1), 57-74.

Eisenhardt, K., & Zbaracki, M. (1992). Strategic decision making. *Strategic Management Journal, 13*(S2), 17-37.

Elbanna, S. (2006). Strategic decision-making: Process perspectives. *International Journal of Management Reviews, 8*(1), 1-20.

Elster, J. (1983). When rationality fails. In Cook, K., & Levi, M. (Eds.), *The Limits of Rationality*. Cambridge, U.K.: Cambridge University Press, 1-51.

Epstein, S. (1994). Integration of the cognitive and psychodynamic unconscious. *American Psychologist, 49*(8), 709-724.

Ferrell, O., & Gresham, L. (1985). A contingency framework for understanding ethical decision making in marketing. *The Journal of Marketing, 49*(3), 87-96.

Finedo, P., & Olsen, D. (2015). An empirical research on the impacts of organisational decision's locus, tasks structure rules, knowledge and IT function's value on ERP system success. *International Journal of Production Research, 53*(8), 2554-2568.

Forbes, D. (2005). The effects of strategic decision making on entrepreneurial self-efficacy. *Entrepreneurship Theory and Practice, 29*(5), 599-626.

Ford, R., & Richardson, W. (1994). Ethical decision making: A review of the emirical literature. *Journal of Business Ethics, 13*, 205-221.

Franke, U. J. (1999). The virtual web as a new entrepreneurial approach to network organizations. *Entrepreneurship and Regional Development, 11*, 203-229.

Frederickson, J. (1986). The strategic decision process and organizational structure. *Academy of Management Review, 11*(2), 280-297.

Fredrickson, J. W. (1984). The comprehensiveness of strategic decision process: Extension, observations, future directions. . *Academy of Managment Journal, 27*(3), 445-466.

Gibson, C. B., & Birkinshaw, J. (2004). The antecedents consequences, and mediating role of organizational ambidexterity. *Academy of Management Journal, 47*(1), 209-226.

Gigerenzer, G. (2000). *Adaptive Thinking: Rationality in the Real World.* New York: Oxford University.

Gigerenzer, G. (2001). Decision making: Nonrational theories. *International Encyclopedia of the Social and Behavioral Sciences, 9*, 3304–3309.

Greve, H. (2013). Microfoundations of management: Behavioral strategies and levels of rationality in organizational action. *Academy of Management Perspectives, 27*(2), 103-119.

Hart, S. (1992). An integrative framework for strategy-making processes. *Acedemy of Management, 17*(2), 327-351.

Hitt, M., & Tyler, B. (1991). Strategic decision models: Integrating different perspectives. *Strategic Management Journal, 12*(5), 327-351.

Hoy, W., & Tarter, C. (2010). Swift and smart decision making: heuristics that work. *International Journal of Educational Management, 24*(4), 351-358.

Johnson, G, Scholes, K., & Whittington, R. (2005). *Exploring corporate strategy.* Financial Times Prentice Hall.

Jones, T. (1991). Ethical decision making by individuals in organizations: An issue-contingent model. *Academy of Management Review, 16*(2), 366-395.

Judge, W., & Miller, A. (1991). Antecedents and outcomes of decision speed in different environmental context. *Academy of Management Journal, 34*(2), 449-463.

Kahnemann, D., & Tversky, A. (1979). Prospect theory: An analysis of decision under risk. *Econometrica: Journal of the Econometric Society, 47*(2), 263-291.

Kalantari, B. (2010). Herbert A. Simon on making decisions: enduring insights and bounded rationality. *Journal of Management History, 16*(4), 509-520.

Koklic, M. K., & Vida, I. (2011). Consumer strategic decision making and choice process: prefabricated house purchase. *International Journal of Consumer Studies, 35*(6), 634-643.

Koopman, P. L., & Pool, J. (1997). Management en esluitvorming in organisaties: Een strategisch perspectief. Assen, Netherlands: Van Gorcum.

Kydd, L., Crawford, M., & Riches, C. (1997). *Professional development for educational management.* UK: McGraw-Hill Education.

Leahey, T. (2003). Herbert A. Simon: Nobel Prize in Economic Sciences, 1978. *American Psychologist, 58*(9), 753.

Levinthal, D. (2011). A behavioral approach to strategy - what's the alternative? *Strategic Management Journal, 32*(13), 1517-1523.

Leiblein, M. J., Reuer, J. J., & Zenger, T. (2018). What makes a decision strategic? *Strategy Science, 3*(4), 558–573.

Lo, K., & Lys, T. (2000). The Ohlson model: contribution to valuation theory, limitations and empirical applications. *Journal of Accounting, Auditing & Finance, 15*(3), 337-367.

Lovallo, D., & Sibony, O. (2010). The case for behavioral strategy. *McKinsey Quarterly, 2*(1), 30-43.

Lyon, D. W., Lumpkin, G. T., & Dess, G. G. (2000). Enhancing entrepreneurial orientation research: Operationalizing and measuring a key strategic decision making process. *Journal of Management, 26*(5), 1055-1085.

Mähring, M., & Keil, M. (2008). Information technology project escalation: A process model. *Decision Sciences, 39*(2), 239-272.

March, J. (1978). Bounded rationality, ambiguity, and the engineering of choice. *The Bell Journal of Economics,* 587-608.

McKenzie, J., van Winkelen, C., & Grewal, S. (2011). Developing organisational decision-making capability: a knowledge manager's guide. *Journal of Knwledge Management, 15*(3), 403-421.

Mintzberg, H., 1973. Strategy-making in three modes. *California Management Review, 16*(2), 44-53.

Mintzberg, H. (1979). *The structuring of organizations: a synthesis of research.* Englewood Cliffs: Prentice Hall.

Mintzberg, H., Raisinghani, D., & Theoret, A. (1976). The structure of "unstructured" decision processes. *Administrative Science Quarterly,* 246-275.

Mitchell, J., Dean, A., & Sharfman, M. (2011). Erratic strategic decisions: When and why managers are inconsistent in strategic decision making. *Strategic Management Journal, 32,* 683-704.

Muren, A. (2012). Optimistic behavior when a decision bias is costly: an experimental test. *Economic Inquiry, 50*(2), 463-469.

Nagel, C. (2014). Behavioral strategy. Thoughts and feelings in the decision-making process. The unconscious and corporate success. *Unternehmenmedien,* 18-21.

Noorderhaven, N. (1995). *Strategic decision making.* Reading, MA, USA: Addison-Wesley.

Nutt, P. C. (1999) Surprising but true: Half the decisions in organizations fail. *Academy of Management Perspectives, 13*(4), 75-90.

Oliveira, A. (2007). Decision-making theories and models: A discussion of rational and psychological decision-making theories and models: The search for a cultural-ethical decision-making model. *EJBO-Electronic Journal of Business Ethics and Organization Studies.*

Oppermann, M., & Chon, K. (1997). Convention participation decision-making process. *Annals of Tourism Research, 24*(1), 178-191.

Papadakis, V., & Barwise, P. (1998). Strategic decisions: An introduction. In V. Papadakis, V., & Barwise, P. (Eds.), *Strategic Decisions.* Berlin, Germany: Springer.

Papadakis, V. M., Lioukas, S., & Chambers, D. (1998). Strategic decision-making processes: the role of management and context. *Strategic Management Journal, 19*(2), 115-147.

Papenhausen, C. (2006). Half full or half empty: The effects of top managers' dispositional optimism on strategic decision-making and firm performance. *University of Massachusetts-Dartmouth.*

Partovi, F. (2007). An analytical model of process choice in the chemical industry. *International Journal of Production Economics, 105*(1), 213-227.

Paul, S., Müller, H., Preiser, R., Lima Neto, FBd., Marwala, T., & De Wilde, P. (2014). Developing a management decision-making model based upon a complexity perspective with refernce to the Bee Algorithm. . *Complexity & Organization, 16*(4), 1-13.

Platt, M., & Huettel, S. (2008). Risky business: the neuroeconomics of decision making under uncertainty. *Nature Neuroscience, 11*(4), 398-403.

Powell, T., Lovallo, D., & Fox, C. (2011). Behavioral strategy. *Strategic Management Journal, 32*(13), 1369-1386.

Sandholm, T. W. (1999). Distributed rational decision making. In Weiss G. (Ed.), *Multiagent systems: a modern approach to distributed artificial intelligence,* Ch. 5, 201-258.

Savage, L. J. (1954). *The Foundations of Statistics.* New York, NY, USA: John Wiley and Sons.

Schwenk, C. R. (1984). Cognitive simplification processes in strategic decision-making. *Strategic Management Journal, 5*(2), 111-128.

Schwenk, C. R. (1988). The cognitive perspective on strategic decision making. *Journal of Management Studies, 25*(1), 41-55.

Schwenk, C. R. (1995). Strategic decision making. *Journal of Management, 21*(3), 471-493.

Shepherd, N. G., & Rudd, J. M. (2014). The influence of context on the strategic decision-making process: A review of the literature. *International Journal of Management Reviews, 16*(3), 340-364.

Shivakumar, R. (2014). How to tell which decisions are strategic. *California Management Review, 56*(3), 78-97.

Simon, H. A. (1960). *The new science of management decision.* New York, USA: Prentice-Hall.

Simon, H. A. (1947). *Administrative behavior; a study of decision-making processes in administrative organization.* (2nd ed.). New York, USA: Macmillan.

Simon, H. A. (1979). Rational decision making in busienss organizations. *American Economic Review, 69*(4), 493-513.

Slovic, P., Finucane, M., Peters, E., & MacGregor, D. (2002). The affect heuristic. In Gilovich, T., Griffin, D., & Kahneman, D. (Eds.), *Heuristics and biases: The psychology of intuitive judgment.* Cambridge, U.K.: Cambridge University Press, 397-420.

Smith, K., Gannon, M., Grimm, C., & Mitchell, T. (1988). Decision making behavior in smaller entrepreneurial and larger professionally managed firms. *Journal of Business Venturing, 3*(3), 223-232.

Staw, B. (1976). Knee-deep in the big muddy: A study of escalating commitment to a chosen course of action. *Organizational Behaviour and Human Performance, 16*(1), 27-44.

Weiss, C. (1982). Policy research in the context of diffuse decision making. *The Journal of Higher Education, 53*(6), 619-639.

Werther, W. B. (1999). Structure-Driven Strategy and Virtual Organization Design. *Business Horizons, 42(2)*, 13-18.

Williams, S. (2002). *Making better business decisions.* Thousand Oaks, CA, USA: Sage Publications. .

Wilson, D. C., Butler, R. J., Cray, D., Hickson, D. J., & Mallory, G. R. (1986). Breaking the bounds of organization in strategic decision making. *Human Relations, 39*(4), 309-331.

Zajonc, R. (1980). Feeling and thinking: Preferences need no inferences. *American Psychologist, 35*(2), 151-175 .

Organizational Learning

Thomas Hellwig, Julia Hormuth, Michael Oberdorfer and Christian Seifermann

Abstract. This article reviews foundational literature in the field of organizational learning, delving into its understanding and various subcategories. We introduce fundamental perspectives on learning within organizations and then explore related concepts like organizational learning capabilities, knowledge acquisition, and innovation. While the benefits of organizational learning are widely recognized, there remain unanswered questions that warrant further research. These include clarifying definitions, understanding its influence on corporate performance, addressing new business developments, and ensuring effective knowledge transfer.

Keywords: Organizational learning, organizational learning capabilities, organizational memory, organizational knowledge, knowledge transfer, innovation, performance

1. Introduction

In today's dynamic and highly competitive economy, it is imperative for companies to cultivate the ability to learn and assimilate knowledge. A company's aptitude for learning—its capacity to acquire, interpret, retain, and apply knowledge—is often seen as a pivotal element for gaining a competitive edge (Kumar et al., 2021; Liao et al., 2017). While extensive research has been conducted on organizational learning, consensus remains elusive regarding its exact definition (Hammoud, 2020), how it differs from organizational learning capabilities, and the most effective strategies for its implementation. Some scholars have investigated how different work environments impact the dissemination of knowledge among individuals, teams, and throughout the organization (Argote & Ingram, 2000; Darr et al., 1995; March, 1991). There's evidence suggesting that a firm's ability to learn can significantly affect its overall performance (Hammoud, 2020; Pérez López et al., 2005; Škerlavaj et al., 2007). Therefore, it can be inferred that companies that master the art of rapid learning and adeptly manage organizational learning processes outperform those less equipped or inclined to learn swiftly.

Driven by the aim to delve deeper into the intricacies and advantages of organizational learning, this article further unpacks concepts of learning, organizational learning, and organizational learning capability, culminating in conclusions and avenues for future research.

2. Learning

In the realm of organizational learning, the concept and meaning of learning has garnered significant attention (Fiol & Lyles, 1985; Huber, 1991; Mynarek et al., 2021). Organizational learning is viewed as a social process, rooted in the interactions that occur across three distinct levels: individual, group, and organizational (Balbastre et al., 2003; Mynarek et al., 2021).

The academic community has debated if learning is solely cognitive or also encompasses behavioral aspects (Easterby-Smith et al., 2000; Hammoud, 2020; Mynarek et al., 2021; Weick, 1991). Proponents of the cognitive-only perspective see learning as the evolution of new insights by adjusting existing beliefs or through the lens of interpreting existing frameworks (Freidlander, 1983; Huber, 1991; Kim, 1993). As expressed by Freidlander (1983), "The essence of learning lies in the conscious recognition of differences and alternatives and in making an informed choice among them. Such choices may involve changing cognitive frameworks rather than behaviors." On the other hand, some scholars believe learning is both cognitive and behavioral. They argue that learning arises from new understandings that consequently influence new behaviors, or the reverse (Argyris, 1977; Crossan et al., 1999; Garvin, 1993; Hammoud, 2020).

Regarding learning modalities, Argyris and Schön (1978, 1996) introduced a notable distinction between two types of organizational learning: single-loop and double-loop. In single-loop learning, a company identifies and remedies past mistakes based on pre-existing standards and norms. Common tools for single-loop learning include performance reports, budgets, and deviation analyses. In contrast, double-loop learning involves regularly revisiting and questioning these norms and standards. While single-loop learning stays the course, double-loop learning adjusts core values, norms, and standards in response to evolving circumstances. This more advanced concept of double-loop learning has been integrated into various learning organization frameworks (e.g., Blackman et al., 2002; Goh, 1998). In recent times, the advantages of double-loop learning, especially in navigating today's dynamic environment, have been highlighted (Jaaron & Backhouse, 2017).

3. Organizational learning

While early discussions around organizational learning began in the 1950s and 1960s (Cyert & March, 1963; March & Simon, 1958), Argote (2011) indicates that the first exhaustive study on the topic was undertaken in 1978 by Argyris and Schön. These scholars formally described organizational learning as a company's ability to detect and rectify mistakes. The concept of the "learning organization" was further popularized by Senge (1990), grabbing the attention of business leaders. Senge characterizes learning organizations as "places where individuals consistently enhance their ability to achieve desired results, where innovative ways of thinking are fostered, where shared goals are pursued freely, and where there's a perpetual drive to foster collaborative learning" (Senge, 1990: 3).

Some researchers have explored organizational learning by associating it with knowledge creation and management. For instance, Calantone et al. (2002) depict organizational learning as a company's initiative to devise strategies for producing and managing organizational knowledge. By acquiring knowledge and utilizing it for decision-making, companies maintain agility and competitiveness in an ever-evolving business landscape (Andreeva & Kianto, 2012; Spicer & Smith, 2006).

Conversely, Calantone et al. (2002) hint at a more proactive dimension of organizational learning, some define it as a shift in an organization's knowledge base, primarily influenced by collective experiences (Argote & Miron-Spektor, 2011; Mynarek et al., 2021). Echoing this, Argote (2011) states, "Organizational learning is the mechanism by which the past shapes the present and future." Argyris provides an added perspective, emphasizing the moments of learning when organizational members pinpoint and rectify errors, and adapt to shifts in both the internal and external business settings. Sinkula et al. (1997) expand on this knowledge creation viewpoint, asserting that besides the generation and application of knowledge, archiving this knowledge for future reference in organizational memory is crucial. In the contemporary business landscape, the necessity for firms to learn from past missteps and achievements, adapt strategies to a rapidly shifting environment, anticipate future challenges, and remain flexible, innovative, and ahead of competitors is undeniable (Kiziloglu, 2015). Consequently, organizational learning is deemed vital for a company's ongoing growth and evolution (Argyris & Schön, 1996; Bhatnagar & Sharma, 2005). Myreteg (2015) perceives organizational learning as a system intrigued by the manner in which information is processed and disseminated within an enterprise.

When seen through this lens, organizational learning, understood as an information processing approach, can be segmented into four distinct phases: (1) knowledge acquisition, (2) knowledge dissemination, (3) knowledge interpretation, and (4) knowledge storage and reuse (Huber, 1991; Garavan, 1997).

1. *Knowledge acquisition* reflects the process of gaining knowledge from different sources, either internal or external. Potential sources could be the firm's own past experiences but also non-organizational experience acquired through others (Huber, 1991; Garavan, 1997). Acquiring learning from others has been referred to as knowledge transfer or vicarious learning (Darr et al., 1995).

2. *Dissemination of knowledge* is an important part of the process as it reflects the distribution of the knowledge within the company. The more effectively the knowledge is disseminated, the more value is added because more employees can make use of it (Huber, 1991; Garvin, 1993; Nonaka & Takeuchi, 1995).

3. *Interpretation of the knowledge* means adding meaning to internalize knowledge by those who can benefit from it within the firm. To fulfill its potential, knowledge needs to be understandable and meaningful for all the different organizational levels. This way, the behaviour impact and resulting effectiveness of organizational learning can be increased (Huber, 1991).

4. *Storage and reutilization of the knowledge* are the steps in which the gained knowledge finds its way to the organization's memory. This organizational memory needs to be accessible for employees as a source for future decisions. For organizational success, the storage of the gained knowledge and its subsequent learning enablement are as important as applying the knowledge in practice for future decision-making (Walsh & Ungson, 1991; Akgün et al., 2007).

Organizational knowledge can be categorized as either explicit or tacit. Tacit knowledge, given its elusive nature, poses challenges for learning (Kogut & Zander, 1992; Nonaka & von Krogh, 2009). Some scholars argue that only explicit knowledge is pertinent to organizational learning because it can be easily communicated and shared (Akinci & Sadler-Smith, 2019; Crossan et al., 1999). However, the prevailing academic perspective stresses the importance of transforming tacit knowledge into explicit form so it can be disseminated among others (Kumar et al., 2021; Nonaka & von Krogh, 2009).

Argote and Ingram (2000) assert that the knowledge of an individual within a firm should be integrated into the organizational structure, allowing other members to access and utilize it. With employee turnover in mind, preserving the accumulated knowledge of individuals by embedding it into the organizational memory becomes crucial. This ensures knowledge retention, even if individuals depart the company. Organizational memory serves as a storehouse of knowledge, housing diverse repositories like social networks, routines, transactive memory systems, and other instruments (Walsh & Ungson, 1991; Stein, 1995; Stein & Zwass, 1995; Wang, 1999; Argote & Ingram, 2000).

Often, a company's capacity for innovation is tied to its ability to learn organizationally (Jiménez-Jiménez & Sanz-Valle, 2011; Kiziloglu, 2015; Templeton et al., 2002). Garvin (1993) views innovation as a by-product of effective organizational learning, noting that stagnation occurs in organizations where learning is absent, with employees reverting to old habits. For genuine innovation, continuous learning and problem-solving are vital. This suggests that companies adept at rapid organizational learning, employing it effectively, will likely outpace and out-innovate their slower-learning counterparts (Goh & Richards, 1997). In a study examining the relationship between organizational learning and innovation, Jiménez-Jiménez & Sanz-Valle (2011) discovered that the impact of organizational learning on innovation surpassed its effect on overall performance. This might indicate that organizational learning primarily boosts performance by enhancing innovation. However, organizational learning doesn't always lead to innovation or enhanced performance. The exact relationship between organizational learning and a company's success remains ambiguous due to various other influencing factors (Vera & Crossan, 2003).

4. Organizational learning capability

Organizational learning has been discussed by various authors, emphasizing the concept of "organizational learning capability" (OLC). This capability is seen as a vital component for future organizational success and competitive advantage (Goh, 2003; Hung & Chou, 2013; Tamayo-Torres et al., 2016). OLC is about an organization's ability to employ appropriate and precise management activities. These activities align with patterns, structures, policies, and processes that support and enhance learning.

Furthermore, they allow organizations to capitalize on prior learnings (Goh, 2003; Jerez-Gomez et al., 2005).

Ussahawanitchakit (2008) describes organizational learning capability as a company's ability to assimilate expertise and experience, integrate this new knowledge with existing knowledge, and store it for future application. Fang and Hsu (2008) pinpoint two key elements in Ussahawanitchakit's definition: the ability to integrate knowledge and the ability to transfer it.

March (1991) outlines two distinct facets of organizational learning capabilities. He terms them as "the exploitation of old certainties" and "the exploration of new possibilities." March associates the idea of exploitation with the gathering of experience and knowledge. Here, detecting and correcting mistakes (as highlighted by Argyris & Schön in 1996) and maintaining organizational routines and memory are deemed essential capabilities for organizational learning:

- *Failure detection and correction:* many organizational learning researchers characterize the abilities of failure detection and correction for future actions as one of the primary capabilities of an organization (Walsh & Ungson, 1991; Prahalad & Hamel, 1994; Nonaka & Takeuchi, 1995; Prieto & Revilla, 2006). According to Fiol & Lyles (1985) defective learning and repeated failure are the results of a lack of these capabilities.

- *Organizational routines and memory:* the other part of March's *"exploitation of old certainties"* is supported by Weick (1991), who considers the development of implementation and operation routines as knowledge stores for organizations. These routines are developed to challenge frequent or structural problems. A number of scholars state that these routines show the organization's aptitudes to store, transfer and recall past experiences. In literature, these aptitudes are also labelled as organizational memory, which is meant to highly simplify employees' access to experiences and gained knowledge (Huber, 1991; Walsh & Ungson, 1991; Lynn et al., 2000). Thus, organizational memory is embedded in a transactive memory system, which describes a shared system that is developed by individuals, groups and organizations to collaboratively encode, save, memorize and recall know-how, knowledge and information (Lewis & Herndon, 2011). Different scholars have found that knowing each other's competencies—in other words, having a transactive memory system—helps team members to develop new knowledge, which can lead to fewer errors, more creativity, more innovation and overall better performance than teams without a transactive memory information system (Liang et al., 1995; Rulke et al., 2000; Faraj & Sproull, 2000; Moreland & Myaskovsky, 2000; Austin, 2003; Lewis, 2004).

Contrarily, exploration focuses on the investigative aspect of organizational learning capabilities. In this context, Prieto and Revilla (2006) view organizational learning as the driving force behind innovation, change, and flexibility. Regarding exploration, scholars have recognized key organizational capabilities such as scanning, problem-solving (Simon, 2000), idea complexity (Van de Ven & Polley, 1992), and organizational renewal (Barr et al., 1992):

- *Scanning:* Collecting information about an organization's external environment and thereby recognizing opportunities and threats is described as scanning capability (Daft & Weick, 1984). Hambrick (1982) suggests that having this capability is required to generate new and proper knowledge. The author furthermore states that scanning the external environment entails research on political changes, the whole supply chain and the competitive landscape, including technological trends which affects the organization. This information is acquired through formless means, including the use of existing contacts and social networks and is done to provide valid knowledge (Singh, 2006).

- *Problem solving:* Cohen and Levinthal (1990) describe problem solving as an important complement to rules and processes, which help to handle frequently repeated issues. In order to solve new upcoming structural problems—for which no existing action plan is available—organizations need the skill to overcome them. This skill, the problem-solving aptitude, is seen as a reflection of an organization's skill to generate and produce new knowledge, as well as interpret, question and redefine already existing knowledge (Cohen & Levinthal, 1990; Singh, 2006).

- *Complexity of ideas:* Having this capability means to originate and generalize new ideas, new perspectives, new solutions, as well as new knowledge through effectively specified management practices and initiatives (Singh, 2006; Alegre & Chiva, 2008). Yeung et al., (1999) state that this organizational learning capability consists of three parts: *"producing (attaining, exploring, finding or purchasing the ideas), generalizing (sharing the ideas intra-organizations), and identifying the learning hindrances (finding and solving the problems that prevent producing and generalizing)."*

- *Organizational renewal:* This capability refers to the competence of organizations to constantly look for new ways to manage and handle barriers to organizational change as well as new approaches and methods for business performance (Huber, 1991; McGill & Slocum, 1993; Argyris & Schön, 1996). Organizational renewal is facilitated by other components that simplify changes in organizations, such as flexibility, adaptability, inclusiveness, teamwork and creativity (Koffman & Senge, 1993; McGill & Slocum, 1993).

Goh and Ryan (2002) examined commonalities in literature about organizational learning capabilities. They pinpointed five essential management methods and organizational traits that support learning within an organization. These are:

- Clear purpose and mission,
- Leadership dedication and empowerment,
- Encouragement of experimentation and provision of rewards,
- Knowledge transfer, and
- Team collaboration and collective problem-solving.

The following figure illustrates the foundational model that Goh and Ryan formulated based on their research with companies listed on the Toronto Stock Exchange (TSE).

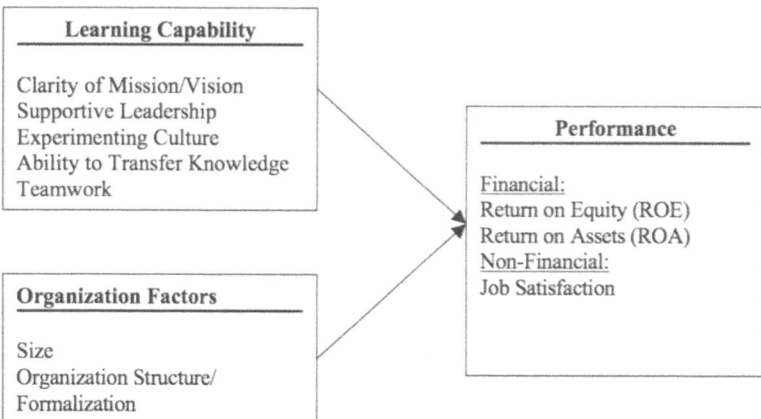

Figure: Conceptual Framework of Learning Capability, Organizational Factors and Performance (Goh and Ryan, 2002).

Based on their research, the authors determined that there's no clear link between a company's financial performance and its learning capabilities. Yet, they did find a positive correlation between learning capability and non-financial performance metrics. Additionally, they observed that as an organization grows in size, its ability to foster learning capabilities tends to diminish.

Comparing the insights from March's 1991 work to Goh and Ryan's 2002 study, some overlapping themes emerge. Of the five key points Goh and Ryan highlighted, knowledge transfer, teamwork, and group problem-solving resonate with aspects of March's framework, specifically organizational routines, memory, problem-solving, and organizational renewal. However, while March emphasized scanning, the intricacy of ideas, and the processes of detecting and rectifying failures, Goh and Ryan stressed the importance of a clear mission, leadership dedication, and empowerment.

Although Goh and Ryan's study did not find a direct relationship between organizational learning capabilities and financial outcomes, these capabilities could still have positive impacts on factors like employee morale and job satisfaction. Their findings suggest that larger organizations might face challenges in cultivating these learning capabilities.

5. Conclusion and research recommendations

The field of organizational learning offers a myriad of perspectives and classifications, often referencing both "organizational learning" and "organizational learning capability." However, understanding the distinction between these two concepts remains a challenge. Organizational learning typically encompasses learning from past experiences, whether they are successes or failures. It primarily focuses on acquiring knowledge, whether from internal or external sources, and interpreting that knowledge. This understanding ensures the knowledge is accessible to the right employees, thereby building an "organizational memory" that can inform future decisions. Furthermore, there's a clear association between a firm's ability to learn and its capacity for innovation, with innovation frequently emerging as a result of adept organizational learning. In the modern competitive business environment, the ability of a company to continuously learn, adapt, and innovate is considered vital for sustained success. As a result, organizations that can learn quickly and apply that learning effectively are typically more innovative, giving them a competitive advantage. Goh & Ryan's 2002 research even indicated that larger companies might struggle to maintain their learning agility, suggesting a potential inverse relationship between a company's size and its ability to learn.

Despite the apparent benefits of quick and efficient organizational learning on overall performance, it doesn't necessarily guarantee better financial results. The direct correlation between organizational learning and company performance is not clear-cut, considering the many other influencing variables. This field presents several opportunities for further study. First, there's a need to provide a clearer distinction between organizational learning and organizational learning capability. Additionally, more research is needed to understand the direct impact of organizational learning on a company's performance. It is also important to examine how companies can adapt their learning capabilities to match technological progress and shifts in the business environment. And with the ever-growing amount of knowledge and experiences available, future research should delve into how to effectively categorize, share, and store knowledge. Strategizing on how to disseminate vital information without overwhelming the recipients will be essential to avoid confusion or distraction stemming from information overload.

References

Akgün, A. E., Keskin, H., Byrne, J. C. & Aren, S. (2007). Emotional and Learning Capability and Their Impact on Product Innovativeness and Firm Performance. *Technovation, Vol. 27*/1, pp. 501-513.

Akinci, C. & Sadler-Smith, E. (2019). Collective Intuition: Implications for Improved Decision Making and Organizational Learning. *British Journal of Management, Vol. 30*/3, pp. 558-577.

Alegre, J. & Chiva, R. (2008). Assessing The Impact of Organizational Learning Capability on Product Innovation Performance: An Empirical Test. *Technovation, Vol. 28*/1, pp. 315-326.

Andreeva, T. & Kianto, A. (2012). Does Knowledge Management Really Matter? Linking Knowledge Management Practices, Competitiveness and Economic Performance. *Journal of Knowledge Management, Vol. 16*/4, pp. 617-636.

Argote, L. (2011). Organizational Learning Research: Past, Present and Future. *Management Learning, Vol. 42*/4, pp. 439-446.

Argote, L. & Ingram, P. (2000). Knowledge Transfer: A Basis for Competitive Advantage in Firms. *Organizational Behavior and Human Decision Processes, Vol. 82*/1, pp. 150-169.

Argote, L. & Miron-Spektor, E. (2011). Organizational Learning: From Experience to Knowledge. *Organization Science, Vol. 22*/1, pp. 1123-1137.

Argyris, C. (1977). Organizational Learning and Management Information Systems. *Accounting, Organizations and Society, Vol. 2*/2, pp. 113-123.

Argyris, C & Schön, D. A. (1978). *Organizational Learning: A theory of Action Perspective.* Reading, Mass: Addison-Wesley Longman Publishing Co.

Argyris, C. & Schön, D. A. (1996). *Organizational Learning II: Theory, Method and Practice.* Reading, MA USA: Addison-Wesley.

Austin, J. (2003). Transactive Memory in Organizational Groups: The Effects of Content, Consensus, Specialization, and Accuracy in Group Performance. *Journal of Applied Psychology, Vol. 88*/5, pp. 866-878.

Balbastre, F., Oltra, V., Martínez, J. F. & Moreno, M. (2003). Individual, Group, and Organizational Learning Levels and Their Interactions: An Integrative Framework. *Management Research Vol. 1*/3, pp. 253-267.

Barr, P. S., Stimpert, J. L. & Huff, A. S. (1992). Cognitive Change, Strategic Action and Organizational Renewal. *Strategic Management Journal, Vol. 13*/1, pp. 15-36.

Bhatnagar, J. & Sharma, A. (2005). The Indian Perspective of Strategic HR Roles And Organizational Learning Capability. *The International Journal of Human Resource Management, Vol. 16*/9, pp.1711-1739.

Blackman, D., Connelly, J. & Henderson, S. (2004). Does Double Loop Learning Create Reliable Knowledge? *The Learning Organization Vol. 11*/1, pp. 11-27.

Calantone, R. J., Cavusgil, S. T. & Zhao, Y. (2002). Learning Orientation, Firm Innovation Capability, and Firm Performance. *Industrial Marketing Management, Vol. 31*/1, pp. 515-524.

Cohen, W. M. & Levinthal, D. A. (1990). Absorptive Capacity: A New Perspective on Learning and Innovation. *Administrative Science Quarterly, Vol. 35*/1, pp. 128-152.

Crossan, M., Lane, H. & White, R. E. (1999). An Organizational Learning Framework: From Intuition to Institution. *Academy of Management Review, Vol. 24*/3, pp. 522-537.

Cyert, R. M. & March, J. G. (1963). *A Behavioral Theory of the Firm.* Englewood Cliffs, New York: Prentice Hall.

Daft, R. L. & Weick, K. E. (1984). Toward a Model of Organizations as Interpretations Systems. *Academy of Management Review, Vol. 9*/2, pp. 284-295.

Darr, E., Argote. L. & Epple, D. (1995). The Acquisition, Transfer, and Depreciation of Knowledge in Service Organizations: Productivity in Franchises. *Management Science, Vol. 41*/11, pp. 1750-1762.

Easterby-Smith, M., Crossan, M. & Niccolini, D. (2000). Organizational Learning: Debates Past, Present and Future. *Journal of Management Studies, Vol. 37*/6, pp. 783-796.

Fang, W. & Hsu, Y. (2008). Intellectual Capital and New Product Development Performance: The Mediating Role of Organizational Learning Capability. *Technological Forecasting & Social Change, Vol. 76*/1, pp. 664-677.

Faraj, S. & Sproull, L. (2000). Coordinating Expertise in Software Development Teams. *Management Science, Vol. 46*/12, pp. 1554-1568.

Fiol, C. M. & Lyles, M. A. (1985). Organizational Learning. *Academy of Management Review, Vol. 10*/4, pp. 803-813.

Freidlander, F. (1983). Patterns of Individual and Organizational Learning. *The Executive Mind, New Insights on Managerial Thought and Action.* San Francisco, CA: Jossey-Bass.

Garavan, T. (1997). The Learning Organization: A Review and Evaluation. *The Learning Organization, Vol. 4*/1, pp. 18-29.

Garvin, D. A. (1993). Building a Learning Organization. *Harvard Business Review, Vol. C.LXXI*/4, p. 78.

Goh, S. C. (1998). Toward a Learning Organization: The Strategic Building Blocks. *SAM Advanced Management Journal, Vol. 63*/2, pp. 15-22.

Goh, S. C. (2003). Improving Organizational Learning Capability: Lessons from two Case Studies. *The Learning Organization, Vol. 10*/4, pp. 216-227.

Goh, S. C. & Ryan, P. J. (2002). Learning Capability, Organization Factors and Firm Performance. *Third European Conference on Organizational Knowledge, Learning and Capabilities.* Athens, Greece, April 5-6, 2002.

Goh, S.C . & ve Richards, G. (1997). Benchmarking the Learning Capability of Organizations. *European Management Journal, Vol. C.XV*/5, p. 581.

Hambrick, D. C. (1982). Environmental Scanning and Organizational Strategy. *Strategic Management Journal, Vol. 3*/2, pp. 159-174.

Hammoud, K. (2020). Organizational Learning and Knowledge Management. *The Modern Society: A Systematic Review. Review of International Comparative Management, Vol 21*/3, pp. 344-353.

Huber, G. P. (1991). Organizational Learning: The Contributing Process and the Literature. *Organization Science, Vol. 2*/1, pp. 88-115.

Hung, K.-P. & Chou, C. (2013). The Impact of Open Innovation on Firm Performance: The Moderating Effects of Internal R&D and Environmental Turbulence. *Technovation, Vol. 33*/10-11, pp. 368-380.

Jaaron, A. A. M. & Backhouse C. J. (2017) : Operationalising "Double-Loop" Learning in Service Organisations: A Systems Approach for Creating Knowledge. *Systemic Practice and Action Research, Vol. 30*, pp. 317-337.

Jerez-Gomez, P., Cespedes-Lorente J. & Valle-Cabrera, R. (2005). Organizational Learning Capability: A Proposal of Measurement. *Journal of Business Research, Vol. 58*/1, pp. 715-725.

Jiménez-Jiménez, D. & Sanz-Valle, R. (2011). Innovation, Organizational Learning and Performance. *Journal of Business Research, Vol. 64*/4, pp. 408-417.

Kim, D. H. (1993). The Link between Individual and Organizational Learning. *Sloan Management Review*, Fall, pp. 37-50.

Kiziloglu, M. (2015). The Effect of Organizational Learning on Firm Innovation Capability: An Investigation in the Banking Sector. Global Business and Management Research: *An International Journal, Vol. 7*/3, pp. 17-33.

Koffman, F. & Senge, P. (1993). The Heart of Learning Organizations. *Organizational Dynamics*, Autumn, pp. 4-23.

Kogut, B. & Zander, U. (1992). Knowledge of the Firm, Combinative Capabilities, and the Replication of Technology. *Organization Science, Vol. 3*/3, pp. 383-397.

Kumar, M., Paul, J., Misra, M. & Romanello, R. (2021). The Creation and Development of Learning Organizations: A Review. *Journal of Knowledge Management, Vol. 25*/10, pp. 2540-2566.

Lewis, K. (2004). Knowledge and Performance in Knowledge-Worker Teams: A Longitudinal Study of Transactive Memory Systems. *Management Science, Vol. 50*/11, pp. 1519-1533.

Lewis, K. & Herndon, B. (2011). Transactive Memory Systems: Current Issues and Future Research Directions. *Organization Science, Vol. 22*/5, pp. 1254-1265.

Liang, D. W., Moreland, R. & Argote, L. (1995). Group Versus Individual Training and Group Performance: The Mediating Role of Transactive Memory. *Personality and Social Psychology Bulletin, Vol. 21*/4, pp. 384-393.

Liao, S. H., Chen, C. C., Hu, D. C., Chung, Y. C. & Yang, M. J. (2017). Developing a Sustainable Competitive Advantage: Absorptive Capacity, Knowledge Transfer and Organizational Learning. *The Journal of Technology Transfer, Vol. 42*/6, pp. 1431-1450.

Lynn, G. S., Reilly, R. R. & Akgün, A. E. (2000). Knowledge Management in New Product Teams: Practices and Outcomes. *IEEE Transactions on Engineering Management, Vol. 47*/2, pp. 221-231.

March, J. G. (1991). Exploration and Exploitation in Organizational Learning. *Organization Science, Vol. 2*/1, pp. 71-87.

March, J. G. & Simon, H. S. (1958). *Organizations.* New York: John Wiley.

McGill, M. E. & Slocum, J. W. (1993). Unlearning the Organization. *Organizational Dynamics*, Autumn, pp. 67-79.

Moreland, R. L. & Myaskovsky, L. (2000). Exploring the Performance Benefits of Group Training: Transactive Memory or Improved Communication? *Organizational Behavior and Human Decision Processes, Vol. 82*/1, pp. 117-133.

Mynarek, F., Steckel, J., Grandpierre, A. & Häring, K. (2021). Das Zusammenspiel individuellen und organisationalen Lernens: Ein Review der neueren Literatur. *Zeitschrift für Arbeitswissenschaft, Vol. 75*/3, p. 1-17.

Myreteg, G. (2015). Organizational Learning and ERP Systems in the Postimplementation Phase: Where Do We Stand? A Literature Review. *Electronic Journal Information Systems Evaluation, Vol. 18*/2, pp. 119-128.

Nonaka, I. & von Krogh, G. (2009). Tacit Knowledge and Knowledge Conversion: Controversy and Advancement in Organizational Knowledge Creation Theory. *Organization Science, Vol. 20*/3, pp. 635-652.

Nonaka, S. & Takeuchi, N. (1995). *The Knowledge Creating Company.* New York: Oxford University Press.

Pérez López, S., Montes Peón, J. M. & Vazquez Ordás, C. J. (2005). Organizational Learning as a Determining Factor in Business Performance. *The Learning Organization, Vo. 12*/3, pp. 227-245.

Prahalad, C. K. & Hamel, G. (1994). Strategy as a Field of Study: Why Search For a New Paradigm? *Strategic Management Journal, Vol. 15*/1, pp. 5-16.

Prieto, I. M. & Revilla, E. (2006). Assessing the Impact of Learning Capability on Business Performance: Empirical Evidence from Spain. *Management Learning, Vol. 37*/4, pp. 499-522.

Rulke, D., Zaheer, S. & Anderson, M. (2000). Sources of Managers' Knowledge of Organizational Capabilities. *Organizational Behavior and Human Decision Processes, Vol. 82*/1, pp. 134-149.

Senge, P. M. (1990): *The Fifth Discipline.* New York, NY: Doubleday.

Simon, H. A. (2000). Observations on the Sciences of Science Learning. *Journal of Applied Developmental Psychology, Vol. 21*/1, pp. 115-121.

Singh, K. (2006). Assessing Organizational Learning in Indian Business Organizations: An Integrated Approach to Learning Organizations. *Second International Conference on Business, Management and Economics*, 15–18 June, İzmir, 3, 33–48.

Sinkula, J. M., Baker W. E. & Noordewier T. A. (1997). Framework for Market-Based Organizational Learning: Linking Values, Knowledge, and Behavior. *Journal of Academy Marketing Science, Vol. 25/4*, pp. 305-318.

Škerlavaj, M., Štemberger, M., Škrinjar, R. & Dimovski, V. (2007). Organizational Learning Culture: The Missing Link between Business Process Change and Organizational Performance. *International Journal of Production Economics, Vol. 106/2*, pp. 346-367.

Spicer, D. P. & Smith, E. S. (2006). Organizational Learning in Small Manufacturing Firms. *International Small Business Journal, Vol. 24/2*, pp. 133-158.

Stein, E. W. (1995). Organization Memory: Review of Concepts and Recommendations for Management. *International Journal of Information Management, Vol. 15/1*, pp. 17-32.

Stein, E. W. & Zwass, V. (1995). Actualizing Organizational Memory with Information System. *Information Systems Research, Vol. 6/2*, pp. 85-117.

Tamayo-Torres, I., Gutiérrez-Gutiérrez, L. J., Llorens-Montes, F. J. & Martínez-López, F. J. (2016). Organizational Learning and Innovation as Sources of Strategic Fit. *Industrial Management & Data Systems, Vol. 116/8*, pp. 1445-1467.

Templeton, G. F., Lewis, B. R. & Snyder, C. A. (2002). Development of a Measure for the Organizational Learning Construct. *Journal of Management Information Systems, Vol. 19/2*, pp. 175-218.

Ussahawanitchakit, P. (2008). Organizational Learning Capability, Organizational Commitment, and Organizational Effectiveness: An Empirical Study of Thai Accounting Firms. *International Journal of Business Strategy, Vol. 8/3*, pp. 1-12.

Van de Ven, A. H. & Polley, D. (1992). Learning While Innovating. *Organization Science, Vol. 3/1*, pp. 92-116.

Vera, D. & Crossan, M. (2003). Organizational Learning and Knowledge Management: Toward an integrative Framework. In *The Blackwell Handbook of Organization Learning and Knowledge Management*. Malden, MA USA: Blackwell Publishing.

Walsh, J. P. & Ungson, G. R. (1991). Organizational Memory. *The Academy of Management Review, Vol. 16/1*, pp. 57–91.

Wang, S. (1999). Organizational Memory Information Systems: A Domain Analysis in the Object-Oriented Paradigm. *Information Resources Management Journal, Vol. 12/2*, pp. 26-35.

Weick, K. E. (1991). The Nontraditional Quality of Organizational Learning. *Organization Science, Vol. 2/1*, pp. 116-124.

Yeung, A. K., Ulrich, D. O., Nason, S. W. & Glinow, M. A. V. (1999). *Organizational Learning Capability*. New York: Oxford University Press.

System Dynamics in Strategic Management

Robert LoBue, Margherita Pasquali and Oliver Vastag

Abstract. System dynamics (SD) is a methodology aimed at providing insights into complex systems across various fields of study. This article offers an overview of the current state of research and the practical significance of SD in strategic management (SM). It endeavors to explore diverse research areas and identify fields of application for SD in SM through a systematic literature review. This is done to determine the extent and means by which SD can add value to SM.

Keywords: system dynamics, strategic management, organizational learning, strategic planning, performance management

1. A brief history of strategic management

Strategic management (SM) has been established as an area of interest for many overlapping disciplines such as economics, sociology, marketing and psychology (Hambrick, 2004). Even though an implicit consensus regarding the essence of understanding for this field exists (Nag, Hambrick, & Chen, 2007), many diverging definitions of SM have been presented. For the purpose of this article, the research domain of SM shall be defined as the field which seeks to examine "the dynamics of the firm's relationship with its environment for which the necessary actions are taken to achieve its goals and/or to increase performance by means of the rational use of resources" (Ronda-Pupo & Guerras-Martin, 2012).

From an historical point of view, SM arose from the application of the strategy concept to organizations, which resulted in the first corporate-level strategy studies around the mid-20th century conducted by Drucker (1954), Chandler (1962) and Ansoff (1965). During the 1970s and 1980s, the field of SM was extended by seeking to balance actions and options between the internal capacities of an organization and its external environment (Andrews 1971; Mintzberg 1987). The conceptualization of this train of thought eventually led to the structured framework of the SWOT matrix (Weihrich, 1982), which can be applied in order to assess the strategic fit of an organization's internal strengths and weaknesses with its external opportunities and threats.

Also during the 1980s, SM developments emphasized the importance of strategic planning to manage the settings for business success in different competitive markets or industries (Cosenz & Noto, 2016). A substantial contribution of this stream of SM research was provided by Porter (1980; 1985) who focused on relating the unique set of competences of a firm to its distinctive market and industry characteristics, with the purpose of creating and sustaining firm competitive advantage. In parallel to Porter's works, SM research also recognized that a wide range of groups and individuals are engaged with and affected by the achievements of an organization. Pointing out that such relations have to be taken into consideration, Freeman (1984; 2004) framed the stakeholder approach towards SM. At this time, the concept of the resource-based view of a firm (Wernerfelt, 1984) also gained importance. This view placed focus on the underlying process of developing competitive advantage by acquiring and managing "a consistent mix of valuable, rare, inimitable and non-substitutable resources and capabilities" (Cosenz & Noto, 2016).

In the following decade of the 1990s, the resource-based view led to further important concepts such as the identification of a firm's core competencies (Hamel & Prahalad, 1994) and the knowledge-based view of the firm (Grant, 1996). These theoretical models were also accompanied by applied planning and control concepts such as the balanced scorecard and the strategy maps presented by Kaplan and Norton (1992; 2000), providing extensions to traditional operational planning and control systems. They have served to illustrate the capacity for a broader concept of performance management and measurement in organizations (Cosenz & Noto, 2016).

2. A brief history of system dynamics

The methodology of system dynamics (SD) was created by J. W. Forrester in the mid-1950s as a technique for simulating complex nonlinear physical and social systems, which enables managers to gain a better understanding of interacting information flows (Forrester, 1958). In this methodology, a system is characterized as a closed-loop feedback structure, which has neither a beginning nor an end. In such a system, a "problem leads to an action, which produces a result that creates future problems and actions" (Forrester, 2009), so that reality is reflected by high inter-relatedness and continuous complexity. According to Forrester's (1968) model description, the system dynamics structure consists of two fundamental classes of variables: level variables and rate variables, which can also be referred to as stock variables and flow variables, respectively (Forrester, 1968).

Combining concepts from various disciplines such as control engineering, cybernetics, and organizational theory (Meadows, 1980), at its inception, SD was applied to industrial company-related problems such as inventory management and factory production output (Forrester, 1958). During the following decades, many scholars have applied SD to additional fields of research such as education policy and public policy (Richardson, 1999; Ghaffarzadegan, Lyneis & Richardson, 2011), taking advantage of its powerful ability in "analyzing the dynamic tendencies of complex systems, that is, what kind of behavioral patterns they may generate over time" (Cosenz & Noto, 2016).

3. System dynamics in strategic management

In its early phase of development, practitioners of SD approached the broader field of management science through a consultant mode (Forrester, 2007), where they studied organizations and suggested recommendations based on tailor-made models from their observations. In the 1980s, SD focused mainly on corporate planning (Hall & Menzies, 1983) and on improving the process of strategy formulation (Morecroft, 1984). From the 1990s onwards, the group model-building (GMB) approach, strongly promoted by Vennix (1996), emerged within the SD application domain (Cosenz & Noto, 2016). This method especially served to increase the involvement of employees and managers in SM and, thus, to internalize lessons concerning dynamic feedback behavior (Forrester, 2007).

Through developing and disseminating widely the concepts of the "learning organization" and "systems thinking", Senge (1990) contributed to the application of SD in SM by emphasizing that companies should enable and facilitate the learning process of their employees in able to continuously transform themselves. Senge (1990) identified five critical organizational disciplines to follow, where the first four including personal mastery, mental models, shared vision and team learning form a core group which are integrated by the fifth discipline of systems thinking.

Following the brief historical summary above, a core aim of this article is to identify the most relevant current streams of research for the topic of SD in SM. As set out in the next sections, a further aim is to shed greater light on these streams of research, by describing how SD can add value directly to the field of SM.

4. Reasons to apply system dynamics methodology to strategic management

Traditional SM approaches are widely recognized as useful for the formulation and execution of competitive strategies. Therefore, their application is common in small and medium sized organization (SMEs) and large multinational corporations (MNCs), alike, but not only in for-profit businesses. SM is also employed in public and not-for-profit organizations. However, over the years, many authors have criticized the effectiveness of applying SM tools to complex adaptive organizations. In particular, one of the major issues that has been considered is the incapability of SM of capturing the dynamism and complexity of managerial decision-making processes (Bisbe & Malagueño, 2012)

Solutions to problems in complex organizations are often limited to past conditions and reliant on historic data. By using traditional SM tools, managers tend to develop mental models and create a picture of the company that may not reflect the current and upcoming reality. These tools offer a static framework that does not consider complex relevant factors influencing the company's future performance, such as delays of participants, uses of intangible resources, non-linearity of activities and other varieties of human behavior. This is particularly crucial for the strategic management of complex projects and for companies that operate in dynamic systems, where a non-systemic framework of dissimilar data, e.g. financial and market-based data, has proven to cause an "illusion of control leading to unsustainable growth and crisis" (Brews & Hunt, 1999). Because of this, Cosenz and Noto (2016) claimed that traditional approaches to SM may prevent managers from completely understanding the structure of the firm and the dynamics in which it operates. Likewise, Sloper et al. (1999) assumed that managers' strategic learning processes can also be hindered by the use of these static approaches.

To overcome this issue for SM, Cosenz and Noto (2016) suggested the combination of SD modelling techniques with traditional management control mechanisms, because SD has been shown to be an appropriate methodology for simulating business performance and for supporting strategic learning processes. Managers would, therefore, be enabled to frame and understand dynamic complex systems, through which they could implement sustainable development strategies (Forrester, 1958). In fact, SD allows managers to analyze the implications of their assumptions, to test what-if analyses, and to challenge their intuitions (Vennix & Gubbels, 1994). Their findings suggest that combining SD modelling and management control systems enhance strategic learning for managers (Cosenz & Noto, 2016) so that they can better:

- identify and measure results, key performance indicators, and strategic resources;
- frame the performance of the company; and, finally,
- develop strategies that drive the sustainable growth of the firm.

Oliva (2003) and Warren (2005) observed that SD models are becoming increasingly common in the analysis of policy and other managerial issues. The strength of these models lies in their capability to "link observable patterns of behavior to micro-level structure and decision-making processes" (Oliva, 2003). The rigorous logic of SD modeling techniques delivers important improvements for strategic management issues and enriches its tools.

Taking the Balanced Scorecard (BSC), one of the most familiar frameworks for strategic performance measurement from the team of Kaplan and Norton (1992), as an example, Akkermans & van Oorschot (2005) recognized evidence that this tool has a number of limitations, such as its:

- focus on unidirectional causality,
- inability to distinguish delays between actions and their impact on performance,
- lack of validation capabilities, and
- insufficient integration of strategic with operational measures.

In order to minimize these shortcomings and to improve approaches towards SM, the authors suggested the use of SD as a modeling tool to develop an organization's BSC. SD provides an "aid to sensitizing policy makers to the feedback cycles and their implications by constructing influence diagrams" (Hall & Menzies, 1983), promoting the use of feedback loops rather than unidirectional causality. In contrast to the BSC, SD places emphasis on the temporal distinction between cause and effect and has mechanisms for rigorous validation. SD also enables the linkage between strategy and operations, while the BSC is relatively weak in its integration between the top strategic leadership level and the lower operational level measures, respectively. The wide scope of SD may enhance the BSC, which is often criticized for being too internally focused. Similarly, Bianchi and Montemaggiore (2008) similarly agreed that developing and validating a BSC with SD modeling and simulation can lead to a scenario in which managers can better understand cause and effect relationships between the variables related to the four BSC perspectives: financial, customer, internal process, and learning and growth.

5. Literature review methodology employed

In order to bring transparency to the approach of reviewing literature for the topic of SD in SM of this article, the following process summary is provided. The literature review was conducted systematically by creating a detailed review protocol to increase the rigor with the aim of ensuring the reproducibility of this study (Tranfield, Denyer, & Smart, 2003; Denyer & Tranfield, 2008). As a first selection criterion for relevant sources, only peer-reviewed academic journals which were ranked 4 or better in the Academic Journal Guide of 2015 (AJG) (Chartered Association of Business Schools) were chosen (Cremer et al., 2015). This closer scope targeted a high relevance and quality standard of the academic articles selected from the AJG subject areas of 'Strategy' and 'Operations Research and Management Science'. From the latter subject area, an exception was allowed and the 'System Dynamics Review' was also included due to its direct focus on the subject of this article. This procedure led to a scope of seven journals for the review process:

- Strategic Management Journal
- Management Science
- Operations Research
- European Journal of Operational Research
- IEEE Transactions on Evolutionary Computation
- Mathematical Programming
- System Dynamics Review

For the next stage in the process, following closely the methodology employed by Cosenz & Noto (2016), a search request was performed in the title, abstract, keywords and full-text fields for the term 'system dynamics' in combination with 'strategic management' in the three academic databases JSTOR, Wiley and ScienceDirect. For the search request in the System Dynamics Review, however, only the title and abstract fields were employed to maintain the desired review focus. This approach led to a search output of an extensive number of articles of potential interest where both terms SD and SM are included. As a final filter, articles which did not place their focus on the application of SD in SM were excluded.

Following Cosenz & Noto (2016) further, articles were screened and eliminated, that:

- only included 'system dynamics' in the reference list to cite other articles,
- briefly mentioned 'system dynamics' without describing the methodology, or
- put emphasis on operational rather than strategic management.

This screening approach brought the final number of journal articles down to a total of 47 for the analytical process which follows in this article.

6. The diffusion of system dynamics in the strategic management field

Employing a thorough analysis of the literature sources remaining from the screened search, specifically relevant trends could be clearly observed among the various theoretical perspectives of strategic management where system dynamics had been applied. Figure 1 shows that about half of the identified article database consists of three main perspectives: organizational learning (20%), strategic planning (20%) and performance management (10%). Strategy formulation (7%) was found, as well, among the perspectives in the other half. The remaining sources (about 43%) are composed of research domains that are bounded by a single organization function or more limited responsibility, such as quality management, supply chain management or investment decision-making.

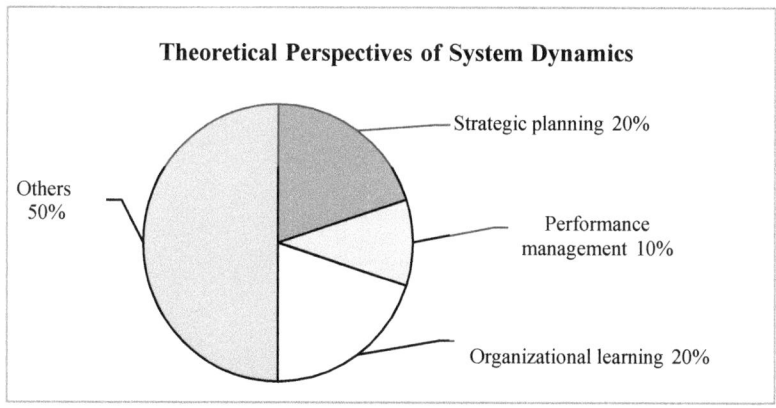

Figure 1: Distribution of the theoretical perspectives of SD in SM.

As illustrated in Figure 2, below, the analysis also determined that SD methodology in the area of SM is used in the articles to a great extent (98%) as a systemic analysis tool which aims to conceptualize "a problematic phenomenon and identifying the underlying structure of the corresponding system, highlighting the causal interconnections between system's variables" (Cosenz & Noto, 2016). 85% of the entire papers have also largely used SD as a technique with the objective of simulating the behavior of the system over time. This simulation approach is utilized in many of the studies as a basis to develop further related research methods such as scenario analysis (15%), strategy testing (8%) and further analysis of various types (19%).

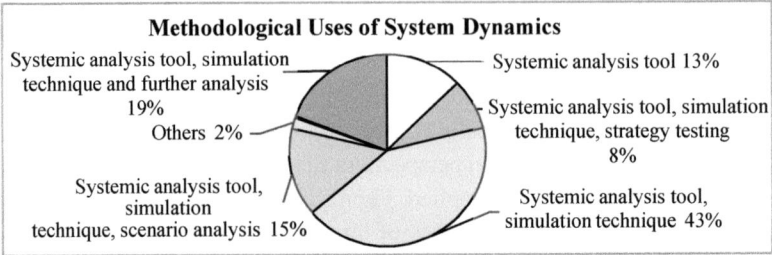

Figure 2: Distribution of the methodological uses of SD.

Figure 3 displays that qualitative methods (73%) have been more widely utilized than quantitative ones (27%). These statistics show that the subject researchers have mostly preferred to conduct their empirical studies through the use of insightful models of observation, written evidence, and discussion, rather than basing them on statistical tests or mathematical data measurements.

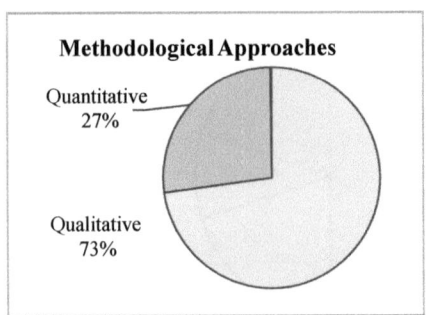

Figure 3: Distribution of the methodological approaches of SD.

As we have seen in the examination of methodological uses, SD is applied in a number of sub-fields within SM. In many articles an overlap of these theoretical perspectives is also observed. Nevertheless, it is possible to clearly categorize the articles according to these perspectives, and, as described above, organizational learning, strategic planning, and performance management are those most explored. These three key perspectives are further discussed in the following sections.

7. Organizational learning

Organizational learning (OL) is related to the continuous process of knowledge acquisition driven by experience occurring within organizations. In the articles taken into consideration, SD has been used as a systemic analysis tool with the objective to explore and analyze mental models in organizations. SD in OL is often supported by simulation techniques, including interactive games (Sterman, 1987; Sterman, 1989 and Senge & Sterman, 1992). In this framework, gaming is used as a direct experiment, in which people play roles in the system to be modeled. Such direct experiments can provide constructive insights but not without limitations. They are generally not able to offer complete feedback on the complex dynamics that characterize tasks in large organizations (Sterman, 1987).

SD has also been widely applied in the fostering of management education. The analytical skills applied in SD allow managers to be more effective in the development of strategies, as they are provided with instruments for dynamic modeling to recognize problems and diagnose their causes by applying feedback processes to their work tasks. Overall, SD facilitates the transfer of managerial insights into the effectiveness of their policies for archetypal situations when applied to individual cases (Graham et al., 1992). This is possible thanks to the extensive use of specific tools, especially causal-loop diagrams (Lane, 1992). These continuous SD feedback loops provide managers with the "decentralized rule-fulfilling decision rules (policies) and the resource systems of the operative levels of corporate systems at a given stage of system evolution" (Merten, 1991).

8. Strategic planning

Another deeply explored perspective within SM is strategic planning (SP), which can be defined in the context of this article as the study of the organizational processes used to analyze, plan and forecast the future outcomes of a strategy (Sharp, 1982). Initially, this topic was treated by contributions focusing on SD as a simulation technique aimed at improving the formulation of strategies (Gottschalk, 1981) or at facilitating policy-making processes during corporate crisis situations (Hall & Menzies, 1983). Subsequently, SD expanded its functionality as a systemic analysis tool and simulation technique through the application to a broader selection of topics within SP, including energy efficiency standards (Ford, 1990), defense expenditure (Coyle, 1992), managers dealing with stagnation (Barlas, Çirak & Duman, 2000), the problem of misperception of feedback (Paich & Sterman, 1993), as well as new methodologies to control complex and hypercomplex socio-economic structures (Brans et al., 1998). More recently, through the use of a dynamic simulation model, Georgiadis and Vlachos (2003) examined the impact of environmental issues on long-term behavior of a single product supply chain.

9. Performance management

The literature review analysis measured that 10% of the sources taken into account deal with the application of SD in the field of performance management (PM), including the processes through which managers align performance with the organization's values, goals and strategy. In the review, the use of SD in PM is traced to Morecroft in 1984, when SD was used as a strategy support tool for evaluating strategy proposals. This was accomplished through the use of scenarios to challenge the intuitions of the management team and to illustrate the policy structure of an organization. More recently, the application of SD for strategic PM has been demonstrated by Lyneis, Cooper & Els (2001) as a way to identify and manage risks and to assess the benefits of organizational changes. Within the framework of PM, the SD methodology can be combined with the more traditional approach of the balanced scorecard. This integration has proven to successfully improve managers' learning and ability to identify causal relationships between policy levers and the performance of the organization (Bianchi & Montemaggiore, 2008; Patel, Chaussalet, & Millard, 2008).

10. Conclusion and outlook

System dynamics provides a universal simulation technique for managers to ameliorate the understanding of interrelated information flows in complex non-linear systems. SD can be applied to different topical areas due to its versatility, which makes it a useful tool for cutting through complexity. SD also combines analytical power (Lane, 1992) and graphical simplicity, requiring little time for completing simulation runs on a computer (Coyle, 1992). These characteristics of SD lead to the conclusion that it can be employed with considerable effectiveness in strategic management.

This article examined the application of SD in the field of SM through a systematic literature review. It showed that many examples of integration approaches for SD in SM have been published. The analysis revealed that SD has primarily been used as a tool for systemic analysis, which is consistent with research showing that systemic analyses are oftentimes the first step for pursuing ongoing studies such as scenario analyses, strategy testing or simulations (Cosenz & Noto, 2016). Additionally, the results indicate that roughly three out of four studies within the research field of SD in SM were conducted with qualitative measures. This underlines most researchers' interest in holistic perception or insight of an organizational system over the quantification of its inter-relationships.

Furthermore, three major theoretical streams of literature for SD in SM were identified. The first theoretical stream, organizational learning, relates to the ongoing knowledge acquisition processes within an organization and stresses that organizations should seek to continuously transform themselves. Management education has been an important topic of interest for OL as the analytical skills applied in SD enable managers to increase their effectiveness and to facilitate knowledge transfer. The second theoretical stream, strategic planning, is directed at the application of SD in SM aimed at facilitating effective policy-making processes. Here, the use of SD simulation techniques proved to be valuable in analyzing, planning and forecasting the future outcomes of a strategy (Sharp, 1982). The third theoretical stream, performance management, seeks to investigate, identify and manage risks that prevent managers from performing their tasks. SD was used to contribute to desired SM outcomes through the use of scenarios to challenge the intuitions of management teams.

Overall, SD has demonstrated its usefulness for the research field of SM in many areas, offering substantial improvements for issues faced in strategic management (Warren, 2005). Since SD models do not contain idealized decision-making processes, but rather seek to describe more accurately how an organization performs, distortions in leaders' intuitive perception can be revealed, in order that better decisions can be drawn so that value can ultimately be added. As has been discussed, the usefulness of SD in at least three fields of SM, such as the above-mentioned areas of

OL, SP and PM, has been widely demonstrated. In a handful of other areas, SD research has been singular and sporadic, such as in quality management, supply chain management, and investment decisions. The opportunity to address future topics for SD in SM can be encouraged by the practical usage of SD models within companies, as many theoretical studies in this research area have been based on business applications. The challenge going forward is, indeed, for SD to become a more widely-used system for companies and other types of organizations. As it is highly challenging to deal with dynamic situations in today's volatile, uncertain, complex, and ambiguous (VUCA) world, it becomes more challenging to determine the potential dynamics and interrelations resulting from these complicated issues, and the appropriate options to solve them. The usage of system dynamics, therefore, presents great potential and should be encouraged to play a greater role in strategic management research inquiries.

References

Akkermans, H. A., & van Oorschot, K. E. (2005). Relevance assumed: A case study of Balanced Scorecard development using system dynamics. *The Journal of the Operational Research Society, Vol. 56*(8), pp. 931-941.

Aksu, I. (2013). System dynamics approach as a tool of strategic cost management. *The International Journal of Social Sciences, Vol. 15*(1), pp. 18-30.

Anderson, E. G. (2001). Managing the impact of high market growth and learning on knowledge worker productivity and service quality. *European Journal of Operational Research, Vol. 134*, pp. 508-524.

Andrews, K. R. (1971). *The Concept of Corporate Strategy*. Homewood, IL USA: Dow Jones-Irwin.

Ansoff, H. I. (1965). *Corporate Strategy: An Analytic Approach to Business Policy for Growth and Expansion*. New York: McGraw Hill.

Ansoff, H. I. (1980,). Strategic issue management. *Strategic Management Journal, Vol. 1*(2), pp.131-148.

Barlas, Y., Çirak, K., & Duman, E. (2000). Dynamic simulation for strategic insurance management. *System Dynamics Review, Vol. 16*(1), pp. 43-58.

Bianchi, C., & Montemaggiore, G. B. (2008). Enhancing strategy design and planning in public utilities through "dynamic" balanced scorecards: insights from a project in a city water company. *System Dynamics Review, Vol. 24*(2), pp. 175-213.

Bisbe, J., & Malagueño, R. (2012). 2012. Using strategic performance measurement systems for strategy formulation: does it work in dynamic environments? *Management Accounting Research, Vol. 23*(4), pp. 296-311.

Brans, J. P., Macharis, C., Kunsch, P. L., Chevalier, A., & Schwaninger, M. (1998). Combining multicriteria decision aid and system dynamics for the control of socio-economic processes. An iterative real-time procedure. *European Journal of Operational Research, Vol. 109*, pp. 428-441.

Brews, P. J., & Hunt, M. R. (1999). Learning to plan and planning to learn: Resolving the planning school/learning school debate. *Strategic Management Journal, Vol. 20*(10), pp. 889-913.

Burchill, G., & Fine, C. H. (1997). Time versus market orientation in product concept development: Empirically-based theory generation. *Management Science, Vol. 43*(4), pp. 465-478.

Chandler, A. (1962). *Strategy and Structure: Chapters in the History of American Industrial Enterprise.* Cambridge, MA USA: MIT Press.

Chartered Association of Business Schools (2015). *Academic Journal Guide of 2015.* https://charteredabs.org/academic-journal-guide-2015-view/.

Cosenz, F., & Noto, G. (2016). Applying system dynamics modelling to strategic management: A literature review. *Systems Research and Behavioral Science*, Published online in Wiley Online Library.

Coyle, R. G. (1983). The technical elements of the system dynamics approach. *European Journal of Operational Research, Vol. 14*, pp. 359-370.

Coyle, R. G. (1992). The optimisation of defence expenditure. *European Journal of Operational Research, Vol. 56*, pp. 304-318.

Cremer, R. D., Laing, A., Galliers, B., & Kiem, A. (2015). *Academic Journal Guide 2015.* London: Association of Business Schools.

Crossland, P., & Smith, F. I. (2002). Value creation in fine arts: A system dynamics model of inverse demand and information cascades. *Strategic Management Journal, Vol. 23*(5), pp. 417-434.

Dangerfield, B. (1992). The system dynamics modelling process DYSMAP2. *European Journal of Operational Research, Vol. 59*, pp. 203-209.

Denyer, D., & Tranfield, D. (2008). Producing a systematic review. In D. Buchanan, *The Sage Handbook of Organizational Research Methods.* London: Sage, pp.671-689.

Drucker, P. (1954). *The Practice of Management.* New York: Harper and Row.

Ford, A. (1990). Estimating the impact of efficiency standards on the uncertainty of the Northwest Electric System. *Operations Research, Vol. 38*(4), pp. 580-597.

Forrester, J. W. (1958). Industrial dynamics - a major breakthrough for decision makers. *Harvard Business Review, Vol. 36*(4), pp. 37-66.

Forrester, J. W. (1968). Industrial dynamics - after the first decade. *Management Science, Vol.14*(7), pp. 398-415.

Forrester, J. W. (2007). System dynamics - a personal view of the first fifty years. *System Dynamics Review, Vol. 23*(2/3), pp. 345-358.

Forrester, J. W. (2009). Some basic concepts in system dynamics. *Sloan School of Management Massachusetts Institute of Technology*, pp. 1-17.

Freeman, R. E. (1984). *Strategic Management: A Stakeholder Approach.* Boston: Pitman.

Freeman, R. E. (2004). The stakeholder approach revisited. *zfwu, Vol. 5*(3), pp. 228-241.

Freeman, R. E., Harrison, J. S., Wicks, A. C., Parmar, B. L., & De Colle, S. (2010). *Stakeholder Theory - The State of the Art.* New York: Cambridge University Press.

Gary, M. S., Kunc, M., Morecroft, J. D., & Rockart, S. F. (2008). System dynamics and strategy. *System Dynamics Review, Vol. 24*(4), pp. 407-429.

Georgiadis, P., & Vlachos, D. (2003). The effect of environmental parameters on product recovery. *European Journal of Operational Research, Vol. 157*, pp. 449-464.

Ghaffarzadegan, N., Lyneis, J., & Richardson, G. P. (2011). How small system dynamics models can help the public policy process. *System Dynamics Review, Vol. 27*(1), pp. 22-44.

Gottschalk, P. (1981). A system dynamics model for long range planning in a railroad. *European Journal of Operational Research, Vol. 14*, pp. 156-162.

Graham, A. K., Morecroft, J. D., Senge, P. M., & Sterman, J. D. (1992). Model-supported case studies for management education. *European Journal of Operational Research, Vol. 59*, pp. 151-166.

Grant, R. M. (1996). Toward a knowledge-based theory of the firm. *Strategic Management Journal, Vol. 17* (Winter Special Issue), pp. 109-122.

Hall, R. I., & Menzies, W. B. (1983). A corporate system model of a sports club: Using simulation as an aid to policy making in a crisis. *Management Science, Vol. 29*(1), pp. 52-64.

Hambrick, D. C. (2004). The disintegration of strategic management: It's time to consolidate our gains. *Strategic Organization, Vol. 2*(1), pp. 91-98.

Hamel, G. (1996). Strategy as revolution. *Harvard Business Review, Vol. 74*(4), pp. 69-82.

Hamel, G., & Prahalad, C. K. (1994). *Competing for the Future.* Boston: Harvard Business School Press.

Isaacs, W., & Senge, P. (1992). Overcoming limits to learning in computer-based learning environments. *European Journal of Operational Research, Vol. 59*, pp. 183-196.

Kahneman, D., Slovic, P., & Tversky, A. (1982). *Judgement Under Uncertainty: Heuristics and Biases.* New York: Cambridge University Press.

Kaplan, R. S., & Norton, D. P. (1992). The Balanced Scorecard - measures that drive performance. *Harvard Business Review, Vol. 70*(1), pp. 71-79.

Kaplan, R. S., & Norton, D. P. (2000). Having trouble with your strategy? Then map it. *Harvard Business Review, Vol 78*(5), pp.167-176.

Lane, D. C. (1992). Modelling as learning: A consultancy methodology for enhancing learning in management teams. *European Journal of Operational Research, Vol. 59*, pp. 64-84.

Lyneis, J. M., Cooper, K. G., & Els, S. A. (2001). Strategic management of complex projects: a case study using system dynamics. *System Dynamics Review, Vol. 17*(3), pp. 237-260.

Marquez, A. C., Bianchi, C., & Gupta, J. N. (2004). Operational and financial effectiveness of e-collaboration tools in supply chain integration. *European Journal of Operational Research, Vol. 159*, pp. 348-363.

Meadows, D. (1980). The unavoidable a priori. In J. Randers, *Elements of the System Dynamics Method*. Waltham, MA USA: Pegasus Communications, pp. 161-240.

Merten, P. P. (1991). Loop-based strategic decision support systems. *Strategic Management Journal, Vol. 12*(5), pp. 371-386.

Merten, P. P., Loffler, R., & Wiedmann, K. P. (1987). Portfolio simulation: A tool to support strategic management. *System Dynamics Review, Vol. 3*(2), pp. 81-101.

Mintzberg, H. (1987). The strategy concept I: Five Ps for strategy. *California Management Review, Vol. 30*(1), pp. 11-24.

Montazemi, A. R., & Chan, L. (1990). An analysis of the structure of expert knowledge. *European Journal of Operational Research, Vol. 45*, pp. 275-292.

Morecroft, J. (1999). Visualising and rehearsing strategy. *Business Strategy Review, Vol. 10*(3), pp. 17-32.

Morecroft, J. D. (1984). Strategy support models. *Strategic Management Journal, Vol. 5*(3), pp.215-229.

Morecroft, J. D. (1985). Rationality in the analysis of behavioral simulation models. *Management Science, Vol. 31*(7), pp. 900-916.

Morecroft, J. D. (1988). System dynamics and microworlds for policymakers. *European Journal of Operational Research, Vol. 35*, pp. 301-320.

Morecroft, J. D. (1992). Executive knowledge, models and learning. *European Journal of Operational Research, Vol. 59*, pp. 9-27.

Nag, R., Hambrick, D. C., & Chen, M.-J. (2007). What is strategic management, really? Inductive derivation of a consensus definition of the field. *Strategic Management Journal, Vol 28*(9), pp. 935-955.

Narchal, R. M. (1988). A simulation model for corporate planning in a steel plant. *European Journal of Operational Research, Vol. 34*, pp. 282-296.

Oliva, R. (2003). Model calibration as a testing strategy for system dynamics models. *European Journal of Operational Research, Vol. 151*, pp. 552-568.

Oliva, R., & Sterman, J. D. (2001). Cutting corners and working overtime: Quality erosion in the service industry. *Management Science, Vol. 47*(7), pp. 894-914.

Oral, M., Malouin, J. L., & Rahn, J. (1981). Formulating technology policy and planning industrial R & D activities. *Management Science, Vol. 27*(11), pp. 1294-1308.

Paich, M., & Sterman, J. D. (1993). Boom, bust, and failures to learn in experimental markets. *Management Science, Vol. 39*(12), pp. 1439-1458.

Patel, B., Chaussalet, T., & Millard, P. (2008). Balancing the NHS balanced scorecard. *European Journal of Operational Research, Vol. 185*, pp. 905-914.

Porter, M. E. (1980). *Competitive Strategy.* New York: The Free Press.

Porter, M. E. (1985). *Competitive Advantage.* New York: The Free Press.

Richardson, G. P. (1999). Reflections for the future of system dynamics. *Journal of the Operational Research Society, Vol. 50*, pp. 440-449.

Richmond, B. (1997). The strategic forum: Aligning objectives, strategy and process. *System Dynamics Review, Vol. 13*(2), pp. 131-148.

Rodrigues, A. G., & Bowers, J. (1996). System dynamics in project management: a comparatative analysis with traditional methods. *System Dynamics Review, Vol. 12*(2), pp. 121-139.

Rodrigues, A. G., & Williams, T. M. (1998). System dynamics in project management: Assessing the impacts of client behaviour on project performance. *The Journal of the Operational Research Society, Vol. 49*(1), pp. 2-15.

Ronda-Pupo, G. A., & Guerras-Martin, L. A. (2012). Dynamics of the evolution of the strategy concept 1962-2008: A Co-word analysis. *Strategic Management Journal, Vol. 33*, pp. 162-188.

Rouwette, E. A., Größler, A., & Vennix, J. A. (2004). Exploring influencing factors on rationality: A literature review of dynamic decision-making studies in system dynamics. *Systems Research and Behavioral Science, Vol. 21*, pp. 351-370.

Senge, P. M. (1990). *The Fifth Discipline: The Art & Practice of the Learning Organization.* New York: Doubleday.

Senge, P. M., & Sterman, J. D. (1992). Systems thinking and organizational learning: Acting locally and thinking globally in the organization of the future. *European Journal of Operational Research, Vol. 59*, pp. 137-150.

Sharp, J. A. (1982). The dynamics of the UK chemical plant investment cycle. *European Journal of Operational Research, Vol. 9*, pp. 238-247.

Simons, R. (1990). The role of management control systems in creating competitive advantage: New perspectives. *Accounting, Organizations and Society, Vol. 15*(1/2), pp. 127-143.

Sloper, P., Linard, K. T., & Paterson, D. (1999). Towards a dynamic feedbac framework for public sector performance management. *Proceedings of the 1999 International System Dynamics Conference.* Wellington: System Dynamics Society.

Sterman, J. (1987). Testing behavioral simulation models by direct experiment. *Management Science, Vol. 33*(12), pp. 1572-1592.

Sterman, J. D. (1989). Modeling managerial behavior: Misperceptions of feedback in a dynamic decision making experiment. *Management Science, Vol. 35*(3), pp. 321-339.

Sterman, J. D. (2000). *Business Dynamics: Systems Thinking and Modeling for a Complex World.* Boston: Irwin/McGraw-Hill.

Sterman, J. D. (2001). System dynamics modelling: Tools for learning in a complex world. *California Management Review, Vol. 43*(4), pp. 8-25.

Sterman, J. D. (2014). Interactive web-based simulations for strategy and sustainability: The MIT Sloan LearningEdge management flight simulators, Part I. *System Dynamics Review, Vol. 30*(1-2), pp. 89-121.

Sterman, J. D., Henderson, R., Beinhocker, E. D., & Newman, L. I. (2007). Getting big too fast: Strategic dynamics with increasing returns and bounded rationality. *Management Science, Vol. 53*(4), pp. 683-696.

Sterman, J. D., Repenning, N. P., & Kofman, F. (1997). Unanticipated side effects of successful quality programs: Exploring a paradox of organizational improvement. *Management Science, Vol. 43*(4) pp. 503-521.

Tranfield, D., Denyer, D., & Smart, P. (2003). Towards a methodology for developing evidence-informed management knowledge by means of systematic review. *British Journal of Management, Vol. 14*, pp. 207-222.

Vennix, J. A. (1996). *Group Model Building: Facilitating Team Learning Using System Dynamics.* Chichester UK: John Wiley and Sons.

Vennix, J. A., & Gubbels, J. W. (1994). Knowledge elicitation in conceptual model building: A case study in modeling a regional Dutch health care system. In J. D. Morecroft, & J. D. Sterman, *Modeling for learning organizations.* Portland, OR USA: Productivity Press, pp. 121-145.

Vennix, J. A., Andersen, D. F., Richardson, G. P., & Rohrbaugh, J. (1992). Model-building for group decision support: Issues and alternatives in knowledge elicitation. *European Journal of Operational Research, Vol. 59*, pp. 28-41.

Walrave, B., van Oorschoot, K. E., Georges, A., & Romme, L. (2011). Getting trapped in the suppression of exploration: A simulation model. *Journal of Management Studies, Vol. 48*(8), pp. 1727-1751.

Warren, K. (2004). Why has feedback sytems thinking struggled to influence strategy and policy formulation? Suggestive evidence, explanations and solutions. *Systems Research and Behavioral Science, Vol. 21*, pp. 331-347.

Warren, K. (2005). Improving strategic management with the fundamental principles of system dynamics. *System Dynamics Review, Vol. 21*(4), pp. 329-350.

Weber, M., & Schwaninger, M. (2002). Transforming an agricultural trade organization: A system-dynamics-based intervention. *System Dynamics Review, Vol. 18*(3), pp. 381-401.

Weihrich, H. (1982). The TOWS analysis - a tool for situational analysis. *Long Range Planning, Vol. 15*(2), pp. 54-66.

Wernerfelt, B. (1984). A resource-based view of the firm. *Strategic Management Journal, Vol. 5*(2), pp. 171-180.

Wolstenholme, E. F. (1982). System dynamics in perspective. *The Journal of the Operational Research Society, Vol. 33*(6), pp. 547-556.

Wunderlich, P., Größler, A., Zimmermann, N., & Vennix, J. A. (2014). Managerial influence on the diffusion of innovations within intra-organizational networks. *System Dynamics Review, Vol. 30*(3), pp. 161-185.

Zahn, E., Dillerup, R., & Schmid, U. (1998). Strategic evaluation of flexible assembly systems on the basis of hard and soft decision criteria. *System Dynamics Review, Vol. 14*(4), pp. 263-284.

Part II:
Tools and Techniques in Strategy

Use of Tools in Strategy

Julius Nausch and Daniel Simonovich

Abstract. This article examines the evolution and current trends in strategy tool usage by delving into literature contributions from the 1950s onwards. Emphasis is placed on tool utilization by managers and executives. Historically, research has concentrated on particular tools, with strategic planning being a primary focus. There's a noticeable surge in interest regarding the analysis of management tools and their real-world implications. Notably, a divergence between theoretical and practical use of these tools is evident, underscoring areas that warrant further research.

Keywords: strategy, strategic tools, use of tools, rational decision-making, decision support

1. Introduction

Corporations often hinge their success on well-defined strategies, leading them to employ executives and strategists tasked with formulating and implementing these plans. Integral to this process is the use of strategy tools which can encompass a range of frameworks, concepts, models, or methods. A myriad of such tools exists, serving to systematize knowledge through structured methodologies, often accompanied by visual aids (Worren, Moore & Elliott, 2002; March, 2006). They aim to bolster knowledge generation while amplifying creativity and efficiency (Stenfors, Tanner & Haapalinna, 2004). At their core, these tools facilitate reasoned decision-making in strategic planning realms (March, 2006).

Broadening the perspective, strategy tools aid managers in making informed decisions, dissecting the business landscape, discerning intricate relationships, predicting forthcoming shifts, and devising solutions for managerial challenges. While many enterprises integrate these tools consistently, a noted decline in tool usage has been observed recently, with larger entities generally employing a broader toolset than their smaller counterparts (Rigby & Bilodeau, 2005).

Despite their significance, academic discourse seldom delves into the use of strategy tools. This article endeavors to bridge this gap by shedding light on the scholarly works surrounding this subject.

2. Scholarly contributions to the field of tool usage in strategy

The domain of strategic management tools has been somewhat under-explored. Existing research has predominantly focused on strategic planning processes and delved into only a handful of tools (Clark, 1997). Strategic planning, a tool in itself, has been extensively studied with its earliest mentions in the 1950s under the title of "long-range planning", featuring prominently in the Harvard Business Review (Ewing, 1956; Wrap, 1957; and others). It wasn't until the mid-1960s that analytical blueprints for strategy creation began to emerge (Ansoff, 1965; Learned et al., 1965).

There was a noticeable dip in strategy tool research during the 1970s and 1980s. Few studies from this era are notable, including one on the efficacy of the portfolio planning tool (Haspeslagh, 1982), and region-specific research in countries like Belgium and Denmark. Another noteworthy trend was the study of tools for non-strategic domains, such as marketing (Kotler, 1984). The tail end of the 1980s, however, saw a renewed interest in practical strategy. Webster et al. (1989) suggested that the disparity between theoretical and practical tool application stemmed from a lack of familiarity with available tools, advocating for greater adoption and enumerating the benefits of strategic planning techniques.

In essence, terms like "methods", "models", "techniques", "frameworks", "methodologies", and "approaches" are synonymous with "tools", all serving to aid decision-making (Clark & Scott, 1999; Rigby, 2001). The fluidity and ever-changing nature of business needs mean that the toolbox of strategic management will always be evolving and never exhaustive (Clark, 1997; Hussey, 1997). Yet, numerous scholars have curated comprehensive tables of these strategic instruments.

The turn of the millennium saw an academic shift towards understanding tool usage from a managerial behavioral standpoint, emphasizing strategy as a human-centric action (Hambrick, 2004; Jarzabkowski, 2004). The efficacy of a tool hinges significantly on the context of its application, with some suggesting the potential redundancy of tools if misapplied (Rigby & Bilodeau, 2007). Studies have shown that managers either gravitate excessively towards specific tools or neglect them entirely, although some tailor tools to meet unique requirements (Vaitkevičius, 2007; Lozeau et al., 2002). This supports the notion of the continuous evolution of tools in response to managerial needs and preferences.

Geographical contexts have also influenced tool usage. Disparities have been observed, for instance, between Malaysia and Hong Kong compared to Australia and Singapore, while similarities exist between the UK and New Zealand (Frost, 2003; Clark & Scott, 1999). Notably, Lithuanian managers showcased a penchant for tools aligned with strategic management methods over those designed for strategic analysis (Vaitkevičius, 2007).

Various scholars have endeavored to compile lists of management tools, examining their application across different companies, sectors, or nations. The following table encapsulates notable contributions in the realm of strategic tool implementation.

Timeframe	Authors	Fields of Interest
1950s and 1960s	Ewing, D. (1956) Payne, B. (1957) Wrap, H. (1957) Platt, W., & Maines, N. (1959) Quinn, J. (1961) Ansoff, H. (1965) Learned, E. et al. (1965) Argenti, J. (1969)	Corporate strategy Strategic planning Strategy formulation Long-range planning Long-range research Management techniques
1970s and 1980s	Reimann, B. C. (1985) Kempner, T. (1987) Caeldries, F., & van Dierdonck, R. (1988) Ackelsberg, R., & Harris, W. C. (1989) Karlöf, B. (1989) Webster, J. L. et al. (1989) Wee, C. et al. (1989)	Country specific tool use Strategic planning Long-range planning Summary of tools Decision-making support
1990s onwards	Schwenk, C. R., & Shrader, C. B. (1993) Armstrong, J.S. & Brodie R. J. (1994) Clark, D. (1997) Clark, D. N., & Scott, J. L. (1999) Rigby, D., & Gillies, C. (2000) Rigby, D. K. (2001) Lozeau, D. et al. (2002) Worren et al. (2002) Frost, F. A. (2003) Jarzabkowski, P. (2004) Stenfors, S. et al. (2004) Rigby, D., & Bilodeau, B. (2005) Whittington, R. (2006) Vaitkevičius, S. (2007) Knott, P. J. (2008) Jarzabowski & Kaplan (2015) Vuorinen et al. (2018) Bellamy et al. (2019) Berisha Qehaja & Kutllovci (2020)	Effect on financial performance Critical review of managers' tool usage Summary of tools Country specific tool use Strategic planning Industry specific tool use Company size specific tool use Decision-making support Tools use of managers and executives Tool selection Tool alteration

Table: Chronological development of selected contributions.

3. Strategic tools and their practices

In the midst of their hectic schedules, characterized by varied tasks and notably social interactions, managers are tasked with making strategic decisions (Stenfors et al., 2004). The tools at their disposal for strategy streamline information and elucidate intricate relationships (Hussey, 1997). Arguably, these tools' standout feature is their adaptability to diverse scenarios and their capacity to enhance communication, fostering a shared perspective (Knott, 2008; Hussey, 1997). Through these tools, managers articulate their vision for the company's trajectory, defining objectives and mapping out strategies to attain them (Reimann, 1985). These tools confer a level of rationality to their decision-making, providing a structured approach to analyze and evaluate strategic alternatives (Grant, 2003; Jarrat & Stiles, 2010; March 2006).

For many managers, the use of strategic tools has become an integral part of their daily operations (Rigby & Bilodeau, 2005). These tools hold potential value for organizations, but their effective utilization requires investment in terms of time and resources (Rigby & Gillies, 2000). Their adaptability allows managers to tailor them to individual or organizational needs (Lozeau, Langley & Denis, 2002; Jarzabkowski & Wilson, 2006). They find utility across the board in both small-scale and large-scale enterprises (Grant, 2003; Frost, 2003). Crucially, for these tools to be effective, every individual employing them within the company must have a comprehensive understanding of their functions and features (Rigby, 2001).

3.1. The goals and outcomes of strategic tools

For a tool to be valuable to an organization, its deployment should align with the right circumstances. Rigby (2001) posits that such tools bolster organizations across five domains: financial outcomes, customer relationships, long-term growth potential, market standing, and cohesive internal integration. While these tools can instill structure and clarity, their effectiveness is heavily contingent on the manager's proficiency in leveraging them (Rigby, 2001; Hodgkinson et al., 2006). Tools often serve managers as catalysts for innovation, communication, and transformation (Knott, 2008). Nonetheless, their presence doesn't guarantee heightened strategic prowess or performance. Some critiques, as highlighted by Haapalinna et al. (2004), encompass issues like tool selection, deployment, and actual utilization.

The strategic journey, from ideation to execution, necessitates cross-collaboration amongst diverse teams. Such diversity, rooted in disparate social and academic backgrounds, can sometimes exacerbate communication disparities, potentially leading to friction. Tools, in this context, emerge as a unifying dialect, streamlining strategic discourse (Stenfors et al., 2007; Kaplan, 2008). Several scholars assert that a tool's efficacy is not solely predicated on its inherent design, but also on the user's skillset, influence, and objectives (Orlikowski & Scott, 2008; Faraj & Azad, 2012). Essentially, tools are wielded with specific intents and results, but their real-world application and the resultant outcomes are steered by the user's discernment and discretion (March, 2006; Orlikowski & Scott, 2008; Orlikowski, 2010).

In essence, strategic tools are managerial aids, geared towards cementing a competitive edge. They're pivotal in fostering company-wide communication, catalyzing collective organizational learning - a significant strategic leverage (Stenfors et al., 2004). Yet, for managers, the journey with these tools is labor-intensive, spanning from tool selection to their seamless integration within the organizational fabric.

3.2. The impact of using tools in strategy

Strategy is fundamentally a social endeavor, where effective execution hinges on seamless communication and collaboration amongst stakeholders. In this context, strategic tools emerge as conduits, harmonizing diverse participants around a unified objective (Hodgkinson et al., 2006; Johnson et al., 2010). Such tools, in strategic proceedings, offer a framework to distill intricate content into digestible insights and bridge social interactions, ensuring everyone is aligned (Stenfors et al., 2004). However, while tools facilitate, the onus of strategizing, instituting, and driving the strategy remains squarely on managers (Hussey, 1997). Tools, as articulated by Knott (2008) and Hussey (1997), don't ideate or enact strategies; they simply assist. Clark & Scott (1999) further delineate that tools primarily perform well in strategic analysis and decision-making phases, rather than in the downstream implementation.

Strategic tools can be tailored to align with organizational or managerial requirements (Lozeau et al., 2002; Jarzabkowski & Wilson, 2006). However, their complexity needs careful management; overly intricate tools could stymie growth and escalate costs (Rigby & Bilodeau, 2005). Assessing the direct influence of a tool is challenging, given that the dividends of strategies typically manifest over extended periods. Directly attributing a tool to a strategy's overarching success or failure is intricate. Nonetheless, March (2006), corroborated by Kaplan (2008), proposes that the quality of communication between a team and its leadership could serve as a proxy to gauge a tool's efficacy.

4. Using tools in strategy

The utilization of management tools is widespread across organizations, though there's been a noted decline in their adoption over time (Rigby & Bilodeau, 2005). The use of these tools is more prevalent in Europe and North America than in Asia, particularly China. Historical data suggests that in 2005, only 39% of Chinese businesses leaned on strategic planning, compared to 96% of other Asian firms (Rigby & Bilodeau, 2005). A clear preference among managers is tools that are straightforward yet efficacious (Knott, 2008). The prevailing wisdom is that tools should conform to a company's system, rather than vice-versa (Rigby & Bilodeau, 2005). Consequently, businesses are nudged towards creating bespoke tools that resonate with their unique context.

A gap emerges when juxtaposing the theoretical application of strategy tools and their real-world usage by managers (Orlikowski, 2010; Vaara & Whittington, 2012). At times, managers may misuse tools, either by misinterpreting data or missing critical factors. Some might weaponize tools to rationalize their decisions, veiling personal or political motives, which may not necessarily align with the company's best interests. This subjective approach can, from a more neutral vantage, lead to tool utilization failures (Mintzberg, 2004; March, 2006).

Ideally, strategy tools should be a bastion in tumultuous or ambiguous situations. However, research underscores a concerning trend: managers seldom tweak their toolkit, even when faced with changing dynamics. The familiar and uncomplicated tools, once ingrained within an organization, seep into its culture. Managers then become reticent to diverge and explore unfamiliar tools, regardless of the surrounding context (Frost, 2003; March, 2006; Stenfors et al., 2007).

More recently, Vuorinen et al. (2018, p. 586) have observed that "the landscape of strategy tools is surprisingly traditional and that contemporary developments in strategic thinking have not yet been transformed into usable tools". Also, managers tend to use tools, which are already known by their workforce and offer a common ground for understanding.

5. Research gaps and future implications in the use of tools

The domain of strategy has been rigorously studied, yet research on strategic management tools lags behind. A more comprehensive exploration of the varied tools and their distinct effects is essential (Hodgkinson et al., 2006). These effects span across various areas, encompassing a company's financial health, its capacity for organizational learning, and the repercussions on managers and their rapport with employees. A deeper probe into the genuine deployment and the tangible outcomes of pivotal tools is warranted (Clark & Scott, 1999). Given that tool usage is molded by political agendas, competencies, and the user's milieu, studies should pivot beyond viewing a company as a single entity and zoom in on its individual members and their engagement with tools.

The research landscape should not only canvas how managers leverage tools routinely but also the degree and manner in which these tools are tailored. Additionally, a significant research gap exists regarding the role of tools during strategy execution. While their frequent use in strategy crafting is recognized, there's potential for their application during the rollout phase, albeit differently. Historically, research has zeroed in on top-tier executives, sidestepping the crucial roles of middle-tier managers and external consultants in the strategy design process (Frost, 2003; Baldridge, Floyd & Markóczy, 2004; Mintzberg, 2004; Whittington, 2007).

In essence, the research horizon extends beyond mere tool utilization. It invites deeper insights into the modus operandi of managers and the ensuing organizational repercussions. While some light has been shed on the tool's role in shaping strategy, the sphere of strategy execution remains largely uncharted.

6. Conclusion

Strategic tools are prevalently employed in strategy design and rollout (Hussey, 1997). They serve managers in three fundamental domains: igniting fresh insights, fostering communication, and propelling change (Knott, 2008). Within corporate confines, anyone interfacing with these tools must grasp and adeptly use them to sidestep the pitfalls of subpar outcomes and consequent resource drain (Webster et al., 1989; Rigby & Gillies, 2000). While executives harness tools to infuse a sense of rationale into decision-making, the tool selection, in particular contexts, is not always rooted in objectivity and can be swayed by personal agendas (March, 2006).

Data-driven studies indicate a widespread adoption of tools by managers across various sectors and geographies (Clark & Scott, 1999; Rigby, 2001; Grant, 2003). However, these tools come with inherent constraints, and many remain under-examined. A significant proportion of leaders vouch for the utility of tools, emphasizing their pivotal role in shaping strategic endeavors. Yet, tools also bring with them intrinsic challenges. To mitigate these, tools should embody three chief qualities: intuitiveness, facilitation of social interplay, and relevance to the prevailing context (Stenfors et al., 2004). Optimal tools pave the way for enhanced shared learning, an invaluable strategic leverage for enterprises.

A lacuna remains in our comprehension of how managers deploy tools and the tangible repercussions thereof, spanning both the strategy creation and its subsequent rollout.

References

Ackelsberg, R. & Harris, W. C. (1989). How Danish companies plan. *Long Range Planning, Vol. 22*(6), pp. 111-116.

Ansoff, H. (1965). *Corporate Strategy.* New York: McGraw-Hill.

Argenti, J. (1969). *Management Techniques.* London: Allen and Unwin.

Argyres, N., & McGahan, A. M. (2002). An interview with Michael Porter. *The Academy of Management Executive, Vol. 16*(2), pp. 43-52.

Armstrong, J. S. & Brodie, R. J. (1994). Effects of portfolio planning methods on decision making: Experimental results. *International Journal of Research in Marketing, Vol. 11*(1), pp. 73-84.

Baldridge, D. C., Floyd, S. W., & Markoczy, L. 2004. Are managers from Mars and academicians from Venus? Toward an understanding of the relationship between academic quality and practical relevance. *Strategic Management Journal, Vol. 25*(11), pp. 1063-1074.

Bellamy, L. C., Amoo, N., Mervyn, K., & Hiddlestone-Mumford, J. (2019). The use of strategy tools and frameworks by SMEs in the strategy formation process. *International Journal of Organizational Analysis, Vol. 27*(2), pp. 337-367.

Berisha Qehaja, A., & Kutllovci, E. (2020). Strategy tools in use: New empirical insights from the strategy-as-practice perspective. *Management: Journal of Contemporary Management Issues, Vol. 25*(1), 145-169.

Caeldries, F. & van Dierdonck, R. (1988). How Belgian Businesses Make Strategic Planning Work. *Long Range Planning, Vol. 21*(2), pp. 41-51.

Clark, D. N. & Scott, J. L. (1999). Strategic level MS/OR tool usage in the United Kingdom and New Zealand: a comparative survey. *Asia-Pacific Journal of Operational Research, Vol. 16*(1), pp. 35-51.

Clark, D. (1997). Strategic management tool usage: a comparative study. *Strategic Change, Vol. 6*(7), pp. 417-427.

Ewing, D. (1956). Looking around: long-range business planning. *Harvard Business Review, Vol. 56*(4), pp. 135-146.

Faraj, S. & Azad, B. (2012). The materiality of technology: An affordance perspective. Materiality and Organizing: Social Interaction in a Technological World, *Vol. 237*(1), pp. 237-258.

Frost, F. A. (2003). The use of strategic tools by small and medium-sized enterprises: An Australasian study. *Strategic Change, Vol. 12*(1), pp. 49-62.

Grant, R. M. (2003). Strategic planning in a turbulent environment: Evidence from the oil majors. *Strategic Management Journal, Vol. 24*(6), pp. 491-517.

Haapalinna, I., Seppälä, T., Stenfors, S., Syrjänen, M. & Tanner, L. (2004). Use of decision support methods in strategy process - executive view. *Helsinki School of Working Papers W-370.*

Hambrick, D. C. (2004). The disintegration of strategic management: it's time to consolidate our gains. *Strategic Organization, Vol. 2*(1), pp. 91-98.

Haspeslagh, P. (1982). Portfolio planning: uses and limits. *Harvard Business Review, Vol. 60*(1), pp. 58-73.

Hodgkinson, G. P., Whittington, R., Johnson, G. & Schwarz, M. (2006). The role of strategy workshops in strategy development processes: Formality, communication, co-ordination and inclusion. *Long Range Planning, Vol. 39*(5), pp. 479-496.

Hussey, D. E. (1997). Glossary of techniques for strategic analysis. *Strategic Change, Vol. 6*(2), pp. 97-115.

Hussey, D. E. (1992). *International Review of Strategic Management 1992 Vol. 3*, Chichester: John Wiley & Sons.

Jarratt, D. & Stiles, D. (2010). How are methodologies and tools framing managers' strategizing practice in competitive strategy development? *British Journal of Management, Vol. 21*(1), pp. 28–44.

Jarzabkowski, P. (2004). Strategy as practice: recursiveness, adaptation, and practices-in-use. *Organization Studies, Vol. 25*(4), pp. 529-560.

Jarzabkowski, P. & Wilson, D. C. (2006). Actionable Strategy Knowledge: A Practice Perspective. *European Management Journal, Vol. 24*(5), pp. 348-367.

Jarzabkowski, P., & Kaplan, S. (2015). Strategy tools-in-use: A framework for understanding "technologies of rationality" in practice. *Strategic management journal, 36*(4), 537-558.

Johnson, G., Prashantham, S., Floyd, S. & Bourque, N. (2010). The ritualization of strategy workshops, *Organization Studies, Vol. 31*(12), pp. 1589–1618.

Kaplan, S. (2008). Framing contests: Strategy making under *uncertainty*. *Organization Science, Vol. 19*(5), pp. 729-752.

Karlöf, B. (1989). *Business Strategy: A Guide to Concepts and Models*. London: Macmillan.

Kempner, T. (1987). *The Penguin Management Handbook* (4th ed.). London: Penguin Books.

Knott, P. J. (2008). Strategy tools: who really uses them? *Journal of Business Strategy, Vol. 29*(5), pp. 26-31.

Kotler, P. & Rath, A. G. (1984). Design: A powerful but neglected strategic tool. *Journal of Business Strategy, Vol. 5*(2), pp. 16-21.

Learned, E., Christensen, C., Andrews, K. & Guth, W. (1965). *Business Policy: Text and Cases*. Homewood, IL USA: Irwin.

Lozeau, D., Langley, A. & Denis, J. L. (2002). The corruption of managerial techniques by organizations. *Human Relations, 55*(5), pp. 537-564.

March, J. G. (2006). Rationality, foolishness, and adaptive intelligence. *Strategic Management Journal, Vol. 27*(3), pp. 201-214.

Mintzberg, H. (1994). The fall and rise of strategic planning. *Harvard Business Review, Vol. 72*(1), pp. 107-114.

Mintzberg H. (2004). *Managers, not MBAs: A Hard Look at the Soft Practice of Managing and Management Development*. Oakland, CA USA: Berrett-Koehler Publishers, p. 24,.

Orlikowski, W.J. (2010). Practice in research: phenomenon, perspective and philosophy. *Cambridge Handbook on Strategy as Practice*, Cambridge University Press, pp. 22–33.

Orlikowski, W.J. & Scott, S.V., (2008). Sociomateriality: Challenging the separation of technology, work and organization, *Academy of Management Annals, Vol. 2*(1), pp. 433-474.

Payne, B. (1957). Steps in long-range planning. *Harvard Business Review, Vol. 35*(2), pp. 95-101.

Platt, W. & Maines, N. (1959). Pretest your long-range plans. *Harvard Business Review, Vol. 37*(1), pp. 119-127.

Porter, M. E. (2008). The five competitive forces that shape strategy. *Harvard Business Review, Vol. 86*(1), pp. 78-93.

Quinn, J. (1961). Long-range planning of industrial research. *Harvard Business Review, Vol. 39(4)*, pp. 88-102.

Reimann, B. C. (1985). Decision support systems: Strategic management tools for the Eighties. *Business Horizions, Vol. 28(5)*, pp. 71-77.

Rigby, D. K. (2001). Putting tools to the test: senior executives rate 25 top management tools. *Strategy & Leadership, Vol. 29*(3), pp. 4-12.

Rigby, D. & Bilodeau, B. (2007). Selecting management tools wisely. *Harvard Business Review, Vol. 85*(12), pp. 20-22.

Rigby, D. & Bilodeau, B. (2005). The Bain 2005 management tool survey. *Strategy & Leadership, Vol. 33*(4), pp. 4-12.

Rigby, D., & Gillies, C. (2000). Making the most out of management tools and techniques: a survey from Bain & Company. *Strategic Change, Vol. 9*(5), pp. 269-274.

Schwenk, C. R. & Shrader, C. B. (1993). Effects of formal strategic planning on financial performance in small firms: A meta-analysis. *Entrepreneurship: Theory and Practice , Vol. 17*(3), pp. 53-65.

Stenfors, S., Tanner, L. & Haapalinna, I. (2004). Executive use of strategy tools: building shared understanding through boundary objects. *Frontiers of E-Business Research*, pp. 635-645.

Vaitkevičius, S. (2007). Application of strategic management tools in Lithuania: Managers' knowledge and experience . *Engineering Economics, Vol. 4*(54), pp. 70-77.

Vuorinen, T., Hakala, H., Kohtamäki, M., & Uusitalo, K. (2018). Mapping the landscape of strategy tools: A review on strategy tools published in leading journals within the past 25 years. *Long Range Planning, Vol. 51*(4), 586-605.

Webster, J. L., Reif, W. E., & Bracker, J. S. (1989). The Manager's guide to strategic planning tools and techniques. *Planning Review, Vol. 17*(6), pp. 4-48.

Wee, C., Farley, J. U. & Lee, S. (1989). Corporate planning takes off in Singapore. *Long Range Planning, Vol. 22*(22), pp. 78-90.

Whittington, R. (2006). Completing the practice turn in strategy research. *Organization Studies, Vol. 27*(5), pp. 613-634.

Whittington, R. (2007). Strategy practice and strategy process: family differences and the sociological eye. *Organization Studies, Vol. 28*(10), pp. 1525–1574.

Worren N., Moore K, Elliott R. (2002). When theories become tools: toward a framework for pragmatic validity. *Human Relations, Vol. 55*(10), pp. 1227–1250.

Wrap, H. (1957). Organization for long-range planning. *Harvard Business Review, Vol. 35*(1), pp. 37-47.

Crafting and Evaluating Strategic Options

Senik Nikoyan and Daniel Simonovich

Abstract. This article delves into the research surrounding the generation and assessment of strategic options, aiming to juxtapose the stances of prominent authors by comparing their contributions in the literature. The review underscores contrasts in the strategy formulation process and highlights varying interpretations about how strategic options are crafted and assessed. The approach to formulating strategic options often hinges on whether strategy is perceived as conceptual or evolutionary in nature. Evaluating these options also has differing viewpoints; it can be perceived as an intrinsic part of strategy crafting, a qualitative or quantitative analysis, or an evaluation of already-implemented strategic choices. Recognizing these biases prompts questions about who actively participates in shaping and evaluating strategic options. A deeper exploration into these behavioral components is necessitated by existing research gaps.

Keywords: Strategy development, Strategy formation process, Strategic options, Strategic planning

1. Introduction

The process of forming a strategy is often depicted in one of two lights: it can be systematic and reasoned, as suggested by Porter (1980), culminating in a structured approach to strategic planning. Conversely, it might be depicted as unpredictable, evolving incrementally over time, as proposed by Braybrooke and Lindblom (1963). These divergent views on strategy profoundly influence the methods of developing and evaluating strategic options. Mintzberg (1994) encapsulates the strategy process as assimilating insights from various sources and melding that knowledge into a forward-looking vision for the business. This procedure encompasses gauging both internal and external elements to devise a strategy. Thompson and Strickland (1998) and Hicks (2011) describe this formation process in stages: initially, multiple strategic alternatives are designed, the optimal choice is put into action, and finally, its performance is analyzed. Thompson et al. (2012) perceive evaluation differently, deeming it an analysis of both internal and external factors that should be factored in when crafting strategic options. Devlin (1989) views evaluation as the initial phase where various strategic alternatives are vetted and prioritized before actual implementation. Before diving deeper into different authors' perspectives on evaluation, it is essential first to understand the concept of crafting, which underpins the strategy-making process.

2. Crafting strategic options

March (2006) stresses that refining the generation of strategic options, termed "exploration", and the skills essential for strategy evaluation and implementation, play a crucial role in shaping an organization's trajectory. The act of crafting, which involves generating strategic alternatives, is often spotlighted as a pivotal phase in the strategy process (Gallagher, Martin & Perrin, 2015). Key influencers in crafting encompass leadership, organizational dynamics, and environmental conditions (Mintzberg, 1987), a sentiment echoed by Devlin (1989) who emphasizes internal and external factors in shaping strategic direction. However, the literature seems sparse in its focus on generating strategic options, a fact pointed out by Gallagher et al. (2015).

Crafting is perceived differently across varied lenses. For instance, Mintzberg (1987) and Levinthal (2011) highlight the piecemeal nature of strategy. A popular approach is strategic planning, which advocates a methodical, object-oriented process. By championing rigorous efforts and leveraging tools and frameworks, this approach leans towards a structured, analytical perspective (Ansoff, 1984; Hax & Majluf, 1988; Porter, 1980; Prahalad & Hamel, 1996). A 2011 survey by Tapino revealed widespread use of such tools, with SWOT analysis and benchmarking being the frontrunners. Porter encapsulates a framework's essence by emphasizing its ability to capture the intricate nuances of a phenomenon using minimal dimensions (Argyres & McGahan, 2002, p. 46). While some scholars highlight the utility of tools in segmenting businesses, others, like Pugh & Bourgeois III (2011) and Hussey (1997), critique their limitations. Notably, Mintzberg (1994) asserts that strategy tools are best suited for pre-established strategies, as the strategy formulation process is more instinctive than linear. Strategy, often foreseen as a future-focused plan, uses past actions as a reference (Mintzberg & Waters, 1985).

Another school of thought accentuates the strategy's bargaining and negotiation facets (Cyert & March, 1963), rooting strategy in crafting by championing idea generation (Markides, 1999; Devlin, 1989; Giraudeau, 2008). In this view, strategy is a construct, blending imagination and embodied realism, to foster strategic domain metaphors (Heracleous & Jacobs, 2008, p. 310).

Prahalad and Hamel (1996) emphasize the harmonization of discipline, inherent in strategic planning, and creativity. Engaging a broader participant pool can stoke creativity and enable active industry influence (von Krogh, Roos & Slocum, 1994; Gibbert, 2004). The idea of a "collective mind" is central to this, fostering spontaneity and flexibility in strategy formulation (von Krogh et al., 1994). March (2006) offers a counterpoint, arguing for a balanced blend of rationality and "exploratory foolishness" in strategic management.

While academic literature signals a tilt from strategic planning towards more intuitive strategies, practical management largely remains rooted in structured planning. This presents a disparity between strategy research and its real-world practice, as observed by scholars like Giraudeau (2008), Whittington & Cailluet (2008), and Jarzabkowski & Wilson (2006).

3. Evaluating strategies

The role of evaluation in strategy work varies among scholars. Thompson et al. (2012) see evaluation as integral to the crafting process. In contrast, Markides (1999), David (1986), and Nasierowski (1989) treat evaluation as a distinct phase following crafting. Additionally, Thompson and Strickland (1998), Hicks (2011), and Mintzberg (1987) interpret evaluation as gauging performance post-strategy implementation. Furthermore, both Szulanski and Amin (2001) and Punt (2014) advocate for continuous assessment in evaluation. Despite these perspectives, Thompson et al. (2012) emphasize that evaluation inherently belongs to the crafting phase due to the inherent assessments made during both internal and external company analyses.

Some scholars lean towards qualitative assessment of strategic options. For instance, Nasierowski (1989) believes decision-makers should leverage advantages to outcompete adversaries, anchoring evaluation in the nuances of market rules and competencies. Others see evaluation as discerning strategic clusters, whereby companies' evaluation traits forecast their likely responses to environmental shifts.

Harrison and Pelletier (1993) argue that evaluation hinges on comparing management choices to determine the most impactful option. Markides (1999) echoes this sentiment, noting that evaluation diminishes uncertainty, especially since corporate culture and structure profoundly influence it. Zahn (1998) differentiates evaluation criteria into "hard" (such as costs and ROI) and "soft" (such as intuitive insights and competitor behavior analysis). King (1983) mirrors this division by categorizing evaluations as a "direct approach" (i.e. hard facts) or an "indirect approach" (i.e. soft facts).

Over time, strategy evaluation has shifted towards analytical and quantitative methods. While David (1986) suggests qualitative methods can be skewed by managerial biases, quantitative methods are believed to reduce such subjectivity. Devlin (1989) charts this evolution from heuristic evaluations to quantifiable approaches, exemplified by using estimated net present values (NPV) to gauge strategic options. Yet, the NPV method is not without critics, notably Hasting (1996), who highlights its dependence on qualitative assumptions. However, blending both qualitative and quantitative assessments is believed to yield superior decision-making results.

Tavana (1995) introduced the Strategic Assessment Model (SAM), which dissects strategic challenges into definable components, aiding decision-makers by quantifying multiple options. Following this, a Multi-Criteria Decision Analysis (MCDA) is established. After shaping strategic scenarios rooted in key uncertainties, options are scored based on anticipated performance. Ram (2012) further refines SAM by integrating perspectives from various decision-makers.

Punt (2014) presents an analogous framework, commencing with identifying uncertainties and then crafting management strategies post-quantification. Contrasting with Ram's MCDA, Punt's model integrates a simulation to verify the feasibility of the proposed strategy. Grundy (2004) underscores the need for frameworks accommodating both premeditated and spontaneous strategies, embracing factors like uncertainty and risk. Concurrently, Priem (1992) introduces a conjoint analysis rooted in statistical regression, focusing on harmonizing strategy, structure, and environmental factors in the decision process.

Mintzberg (1987) ties the evaluation of strategic options directly to organizational performance, positioning it as a subsequent post-implementation phase. Performance metrics, including indicators like net profit and stock price, serve as the evaluation foundation (Glueck, 1980). Thompson and Strickland (1998) and Hicks (2011) share this perspective. Evaluation can be split into internal and external facets, with Hicks (2011) using tools such as "the balanced scorecard" from Kaplan and Norton (1996) for comprehensive assessment. Gallagher, Martin, and Perrin (2015) propose an evaluation matrix that gauges strategy efficacy against capital allocation and risk, while factoring in upcoming uncertainties.

Echoing Szulanski and Amin (2001), Punt (2014) champions continuous assessment in strategy evaluation. Hicks (2011) enriches this by embedding feedback mechanisms at every stage to enhance strategy execution. The following table provides a comparison of various authors' perspectives on evaluation.

Evaluation as part of strategy crafting	Hofer (1975), Thompson et al. (2012)
Qualitative evaluation of strategic options	Glueck (1980), King (1983), Harrison and Pelletier (1993), Markides (1999), Nasierowski (1989), Zahn (1998)
Quantitative evaluation of strategic options	David (1986), Devlin (1989), Grundy (2004), Hasting (1996), Priem (1992), Punt (2014), Ram (2012), Tavana (1995)
Performance evaluation of implemented strategies	Gallagher, Martin and Perrin (2015), Glueck (1980), Hicks (2011), Mintzberg (1987), Thompson and Strickland (1998)
Continuous evaluation	Hicks (2011), Punt (2014), Szulanski and Amin (2001)

Table: Comparison of various authors' views on evaluation.

4. Responsibility for crafting and evaluation

Mintzberg and Waters (1985) categorize strategies as either emergent or deliberate. Emergent strategies refer to an adaptable, spontaneous approach, while deliberate strategies follow a predetermined plan, aiming for consistency between intention and execution. While emergent strategies align with a bottom-up philosophy, deliberate strategies are top-down, spearheaded by senior management. This dichotomy prompts the question: who is responsible for crafting and evaluating strategic choices? (Prahalad and Hamel, 1996). Traditionally, top leadership, particularly the CEO, is viewed as pivotal in formulating strategy (Priem, 1992; Devlin 1989; Hussey, 1997). Bourgeois and Brodwin (1984) describe top management's role in two ways: as a "commander" who deliberately sets out strategy for the organization or as a "sponsor" who endorses emergent strategies. Hart and Banbury (1994) further segment top management's role into five roles:

- *Command*: Aligning with the "commander" role highlighted by Bourgeois and Brodwin.
- *Symbolic*: Where top management serves as a mentor.
- *Rational*: Top management is viewed authoritatively as the leader.

- *Transactive*: Top management acts as a collaborator or enabler.
- *Generative*: This mirrors Bourgeois' and Brodwin's (1984) "sponsor" perspective.

Pugh and Bourgeois III (2011) propose a model that casts the CEO as a mediator, resonating with Hax and Majluf (1988). They argue that while CEOs are responsible for setting the overall direction, selecting specific strategic options is left to the broader team. Contrary to this, Mintzberg (1994) and Lorange (1980) suggest that top management, especially the CEO, should maintain a distance from the granular strategy-making process, adopting more of a visionary or design-centric role. Supporting this perspective, Giraudeau (2008) likens managers to craftsmen, emphasizing the creative aspect of strategy.

Although firms may benefit from clear guidance by senior leaders, it is also argued that organizational members should operate as "entrepreneurs," exhibiting independence and spearheading new initiatives (Burgelman, 1983). In contrast, Guth and MacMillan (1986) view employees as "good soldiers," primarily executing the vision set by upper management. Nordqvist and Melin (2008) describe corporate leaders as "social architects," directing long-term strategic planning within their organizations.

In summary, the debate over who is responsible for devising and assessing strategy is multifaceted, and one's stance largely depends on their fundamental understanding of what strategy entails.

5. Research gap and future implications

In the earlier section on crafting strategic options, we highlighted the need for further research to bridge the gap between academic insights and practical strategy implementation (Jarzabkowski and Wilson, 2006; Whittington and Cailluet, 2008). When it comes to evaluating strategies, the amalgamation of quantitative and qualitative methods still presents a significant area for investigation (Nasierowski, 1989). The question of "who drives strategy?" especially in terms of behavioral elements within the strategy formation, is another dimension warranting deeper scrutiny.

Biases play a potent role in the strategy formulation process (Greve, 2013; Powell, Lovallo, and Fox, 2011). Yet, there's a noticeable research void concerning how these biases affect both the crafting and evaluation of strategies. While incorporating quantitative models in evaluations might mitigate bias influences, there's still an evident neglect in accounting for psychological elements (Lovallo and Sibony, 2010). As for crafting, biases can skew the creation of strategic alternatives. It is crucial to utilize tools that not only acknowledge emotional factors but also aim to neutralize behavioral biases' impacts (Hodgkinson and Healey, 2011; Levinthal, 2011).

6. Conclusion

In discussing methods for generating strategic options, two distinct approaches emerge: one emphasizes a structured crafting process based on strategic frameworks, while the other champions a more creative, imaginative approach (Thompson et al., 2012). Despite Szulanski's and Amin's (2001) observation that crafting strategy has not been a major focal point in academia, recent studies and academic discussions have not resulted in a unified understanding of how best to generate strategic alternatives.

The strategy evaluation process has evolved over time, transitioning from primarily qualitative methods to more quantitative ones. Both methods offer unique benefits and drawbacks, as explored in this review. A blended approach, integrating both qualitative and quantitative evaluations, appears to be the most balanced and effective solution (Ram, 2012). Recent thought has also emphasized the importance of ongoing performance evaluations to gauge the efficacy of implemented strategic options (Szulanski and Amin, 2001; Hicks, 2011; Punt, 2014). Furthermore, considering the impact of behavioral biases on strategy crafting and evaluation underscores the importance of understanding the psychological dynamics of key players involved, including top and middle management and consultants.

Though the presented insights and viewpoints often seem contradictory, a prevailing agreement among scholars is the pivotal role of the crafting and evaluation phases in the strategy formation process (Gallagher et al., 2015).

References

Argyres, N. & McGahan, A. M. (2002). An interview with Michael Porter. *Academy of Management Executive, 16*(2), 43-51.

Allio, R. J. (2006). Strategic thinking: the ten big ideas. *Strategy & Leadership, 34*(4), 4-13.

Ansoff, I. (1984). *Implanting Strategic Management.* Englewood Cliffs, Prentice Hall, New Jersey.

Bourgeois, L. J. & Brodwin, D. R. (1984). Strategic implementation: Five approaches to an elusive phenomenon. *Strategic Management Journal*, (3), 241-264.

Braybrooke, D. & Lindblom, C. E. (1963). *A Strategy of Decision*. Free Press, New York.

Burgelman, R. (1983). A model of interaction of strategic behavior, corporate context, and the concept of strategy. *Academy of Management Review, 8*, 61-70.

Clark, D. N. (1992). A literature analysis of the use of management science tools in strategic planning. *Journal of the Operational Research Society*, 43(9), 859-870.

Cyert, R. M. & March, J. G. (1963). *A Behavioral Theory of the Firm*. Prentice Hall, Englewood Cliffs, New Jersey.

David, F. R. (1986). The strategic planning matrix - A quantitative approach. *Long Range Planning, 19*(5), 102-107.

Devlin, G. (1989). The effective development and evaluation of strategic options. *European Management Journal, 7*(10), 97-102.

Duggan, W. (2007). *Strategic Intuition*, Columbia Business School Publishing, New York, NY.

Gallagher, M. A., Martin, K. M., & Perrin, A. M. (2015). Alternative strategies: A systematic approach to generate strategy options. *Technological Forecasting & Social Change, 101*, 328-337.

Giraudeau, M. (2008). The drafts of strategy: Opening up plans and their uses. *Long Range Planning, 41*(3), 291-308.

Glueck, W. F. (1980). *Business Policy and Strategic Management*. McGraw-Hill, New York.

Greve, H. R. (2013). Symposium. Microfoundations of management: Behavioral strategies and levels of rationality in organizational action. *The Academy of Management Perspectives, 27*(2), 103-119.

Grundy, G. (2004). Rejuvenating strategic management: The Strategic Option Grid. *Strategic Change, 13*, 111-123.

Guth, W. and MacMillan, I. (1986). Strategy implementation versus middle management self-interest. *Strategic Management Journal, 7*, 313-327.

Harrison, E. F. & Pelletier, M. A. (1993). A typology of strategic choice. *Technological Forecasting and Social Change, 44*, 245-263.

Hart, S. & Banbury, C. (1994). How strategy-making processes can make a difference. *Strategic Management Journal, 15*, 251-269.

Hastings, S. (1996). A strategy evaluation model for management. *Management Decision, 34*(1), 25-34.

Hax, A. C. & Majluf, N. S. (1988). The concept of strategy and the strategy formation process. *Interfaces, 18*(3), 99-109.

Heracleous, L. & Jacobs, C. D. (2008). Crafting strategy: The role of embodied metaphors. *Long Range Planning, 41*(3), 309-325.

Hicks, K. & Mosely, J. L. (2011). Developing and executing strategy: Using the Balanced Scorecard for alignment and accountability. *Performance Improvement, 50*(8), 41-47.

Hussey, D. E. (1997). Glossary of techniques for strategic analysis. *Strategic Change, 6*, 97-115.

Jarzabkowski, P. & Wilson, D. C. (2006). Actionable strategy knowledge: A practice perspective. *Management Journal, 24*(5), 348–367.

Kaplan, R. & Norton, D. (1996). Using the Balanced Scorecard as a Strategic Management System. *Harvard Business Review, 74*(1), 75-85.

King, W. R. (1983). Evaluating strategic planning systems. *Strategic Management Journal, 4*, 263-277.

Levinthal, D. A. (2011). A behavioral approach to strategy - what's the alternative? *Strategic Management Journal, 32*, 1517-1523.

Lovallo, D. & Sibony, O. (2010). The case for behavioral strategy. *McKinsey Quarterly, 2*(1), 30-43.

March, J. G. (2006): Rationality, foolishness, and adaptive intelligence. *Strategic Management Journal, 27*, 201–214.

Markides, C. (1999). Six principles of breakthrough strategy. *Business Strategy Review, 10*(2), 1-10.

Mintzberg, H. (1987). Crafting strategy. *Harvard Business Review, 65*(4), 66-75.

Mintzberg, H. (1990). *Strategy Formation: Schools of Thoughts. Perspectives on Strategic Management.* The Free Press, New York.

Mintzberg, H. (1994): The fall and rise of strategic planning. *Harvard Business Review, 72*(1), 107-114.

Mintzberg, H. & Waters, J. A. (1985). Of strategies, deliberate and emergent. *Strategic Management Journal, 6*(3), 257-272.

Nasierowski, W. (1989). Methods to evaluate and select strategic slans: A review of concepts. *Management Research News, 12*(8), 5-19.

Nordqvist, M. & Melin, L. (2008). Strategic planning champions: Social craftspersons, artful interpreters and known strangers. *Long Range Planning, 41*, 326-344.

Porter, M. E. (1980). *Competitive Strategy: Techniques for Analyzing Industries and Competitors*. Free Press, New York.

Powell, T. C. & Lovallo, D. & Fox, C. R. (2011). Behavioral strategy. *Strategic Management Journal, 32*, 1369-1386.

Prahalad, C. K. & Hamel, G. (1996). *Competing for the Future*. Harvard Business Review Press, Boston, Massachusetts.

Priem, R. L. (1992). An application of metric conjoint analysis for the evaluation of top managers' individual strategic decision making processes: A research note. *Strategic Management Journal, 13*, 143-151.

Pugh, J. & Bourgeois III, L. J. (2011). "Doing" strategy. *Journal of Strategy and Management, 4*(2), 172-179.

Punt, A. E. & Haddon, M. & Butterworth, D. S. & de Moor, C. L. & De Oliveira, J. A. A. (2016). Management strategy evaluation: Best practices. *Fish and Fisheries, 17*, 303-334.

Ram, C. & Montibeller, G. (2013). Exploring the impact of evaluating strategic options in a scenario-based multi-criteria framework. *Technological Forecasting & Social Change, 80*, 657–672.

Raynor, M. E. (2007). Strategic options: a new tool for managing in turbulent environments. *Business Strategy Series, 9*(1), 21-29.

Roos, J. & Victor, B. (1999). Towards a model of strategy making as serious play. *European Management Journal, 17*(4), 348-355.

Szulanski, G. & Amin, K. (2001). Learning to make strategy: Balancing discipline and imagination. *Long Range Planning, 34*, 537-556.

Tavana, M. & Banerjee, S. (1995). Strategic Assessment Model (SAM): A multiple criteria decision support system for evaluation of strategic alternatives. *Decision Sciences, 26*(1), 119-143.

Thompson, A. A. & Strickland, A. J. (1998). *Crafting and Implementing Strategy: Text and Readings.* Boston, McGraw-Hill.

Thompson, A. A.; Gamble, J. E.; Peteraf, M. A. & Strickland, A. J. (2012). *Crafting and Executing Strategy: Concepts and Cases.* New York, McGraw-Hill.

von Krogh, G.; Roos, J. & Slocum, K. (1994). An essay on corporate epistemology. *Strategic Management Journal, 15*, 53-71.

Whittington, R. & Cailluet, L. (2008). The crafts of strategy. Special issue introduction by the guest editors. *Long Range Planning, 41*(3), 241-247.

Zahn, E.; Dillerup, R. & Schmid, U. (1998). Strategic evaluation of flexible assembly systems on the basis of hard and soft decision criteria. *System Dynamics Review, 14*(4), 263-284.

Using 'Simple Rules' in Strategic Management

Madlon Peter and Deborah Chaya Simonovich

Abstract. This article provides a brief review of the concept of "simple rules" in strategy, as first introduced by Eisenhardt and Sull in 2001, examining its current motivation, processes, and key considerations for successful adoption. Drawing on the transformation of past experiences into heuristics, we explore how simple rules can help firms simplify and improve decision-making. However, effective implementation requires careful consideration of the appropriate level of centralization, speed, and structure in decision-making, as well as critical conditions for success. Our analysis highlights the different types of simple rules and provides exemplifications from the pioneering and follow-on work of Eisenhardt and Sull and their collaborators and peers. Despite the potential benefits, we identify gaps and open questions that require further research for broader adoption of the simple rules approach.

Keywords: simple rules, heuristics, experience, decision-making, uncertainty, behavioral strategy

1. Introduction

In today's hypercompetitive business environment, companies must adapt their operations to the pace of change and make fast decisions to remain relevant. As a result, strategies need to be formulated and re-formulated regularly to align with shifting market demands. To navigate this complex environment, Eisenhardt's & Sull's (2001) concept of "simple rules" provides a framework for guiding strategic decision-making. This approach involves targeting critical issues and providing simple heuristics on what needs to be done and how to do it. Since its inception, scholars have explored the application of simple rules in various business contexts, including business model innovation (Sun et al., 2018; Ellonen et al., 2021), CSR strategies (Goby & Karimova, 2021), and crisis management, such as the Covid-19 pandemic (Furr & Eisenhardt, 2021). This article reviews relevant contributions that establish the case for simplicity in strategy and provides practical steps, examples, and key success factors for implementing simple rules effectively. However, while the potential benefits of simple rules are clear, significant gaps remain in understanding how to integrate them into practice. This article concludes by identifying key areas for further research and practical adoption of the simple rules concept.

2. The idea for simplicity in strategic decision-making

Effective and timely decision-making is essential for organizations in competitive markets. Studies have shown that simple models, relying on limited data, can be as precise or even more so than intricate ones (Makridakis & Hibon, 2000; Andersson, Edman & Ekman, 2005). Consequently, a strategy grounded in simplicity, as opposed to an intricate amalgamation of data and solution choices, could yield superior performance outcomes. Some experts contend that experienced managers, due to their familiarity with their operational context, can adeptly choose the best strategy for a specific scenario (Rieskamp & Otto, 2006; Scheibehenne & Bröder, 2007). Scheibehenne et al. (2007) posited that managers are swayed by "recognition information" (p. 417), having cultivated straightforward heuristics from their experiences. Yet, in numerous sectors, decision-making is complicated by factors like competitors, rapid product lifecycles, and global events. These complexities can diminish the impact of recognition information, potentially constraining the application of simple heuristics.

2.1. Organizational learning and heuristics

Organizational processes play a pivotal role in executing a firm's strategy and delivering value to both the company and its stakeholders (Sapienza et al., 2006; Davis et al., 2007). Essential processes like product development (Brown & Eisenhardt, 1997), acquisitions (Graebner, 2004; Vermeulen & Barkema, 2001), and alliances (Hoang & Rothaermel, 2005; Hallen, 2008) enable businesses to allocate and structure resources, fostering growth and profitability. For sustained competitiveness in fluid markets, companies must perpetually refine their processes in line with strategic imperatives, fostering learning and knowledge expansion (Teece et al., 1997; Eisenhardt & Martin, 2000).

Argote (1999) suggests that many companies embed learning within their operations by drawing from past errors and repetitive tasks over extended periods, facilitating a better grasp of present business needs and the urgency to evolve traditional practices. Yet, Bingham and Eisenhardt (2011) highlight a noticeable divide between the requisite learning and assimilating the insights from such learning into organizational procedures.

They advocate for simple rules or heuristics that afford flexible pathways for processes like product innovation or global expansion. In environments marked by resource constraints, limited time, scant information, and limited capacity, these heuristics provide valuable alternatives (Newell & Simon, 1972). As Hutchinson and Gigerenzer (2005) note, "simple heuristics excel at prompt decision-making even with sparse data" (p. 97), empowering companies to swiftly delineate decision biases and activate strategic options (Davis et al., 2007). Through the adoption of simple rules, businesses can better align their operations with overarching strategies, carving out a competitive edge.

2.2. Levels of centralization, speed and structure in strategic decision-making

The rapid shifts in demand, competition, and technological innovations can quickly render information outdated, leading to missed chances and significant blunders (Bourgeois & Eisenhardt, 1988; Eisenhardt, 1989, 1990, 2013). Consequently, there have been various recommendations for speedy decision-making. In an early work, Vroom and Yetton (1973) proposed that centralizing authority and reducing broader participation can hasten decisions. This perspective argues that extensive participation is counterproductive in high-speed environments, slowing down the decision-making process (Vroom & Yetton, 1973; March & Olsen, 1976; Staw, Sandelands & Dutton, 1981; Mintzberg et al., 1976). Other strategies underscore simplicity in decision-making, advocating for minimal viewpoints and data sources (Fredrickson & Mitchell, 1984; Schweiger et al., 1986). Yet, it is not just individual managers; teams can also devise swift strategies to challenge centralization and bolster entrepreneurial performance (Eisenhardt & Bourgeois, 1988; Eisenhardt et al., 1997).

Eisenhardt (1990) pinpoints the temporal aspect of decision-making, differentiating between rapid and deliberate decision-makers. The latter group invests in detailed planning and future forecasting, settling on one choice after thorough vetting and discarding other options, emphasizing data-backed justifications and seeking counsel from novices. Such a decision-making style might result in ill-fitting choices grounded in shaky assumptions. On the contrary, swift decision-makers prioritize current, real-time data, continually assessing both external and internal conditions to grasp the immediate business landscape. This up-to-the-minute information, defined as data "with minimal delays between events and their reporting" (Eisenhardt, 1989, p. 549), is vital. In this approach, seasoned advisors weigh in on multiple scenarios (Eisenhardt, 2013), with frequent meetings addressing internal and external developments. Some scholars, however, critique this speed, suggesting hasty decisions can be error-prone, demanding more time, effort, and leading to subpar outcomes (Weick, 1998; Okhuysen & Eisenhardt, 2002).

There's a broader conversation on the balance between structure and flexibility in decision-making (Hargadon & Sutton, 1997; Rindova & Kotha, 2001; Rothaermel et al., 2006; Owen-Smith & Powell, 2003). Insufficient structure can lead to ambiguity and poor outcomes (Weick, 1993; Okhuysen et al., 2002; Baker & Nelson, 2005), whereas excessive structure might stifle adaptability, critical for seizing emerging opportunities (Miller & Friesen, 1980; Siggelkow, 2001; Martin & Eisenhardt, 2010). Research indicates that firms in volatile settings thrive with reduced structure (Eisenhardt & Martin, 2000; Rowley et al., 2000), while those in stable conditions benefit from a more established framework (Pisano, 1994; Rivkin & Siggelkow, 2003). Even when spontaneity is needed, a degree of guidance ensures structured outcomes and superior performance (Davis et al., 2009; Eisenhardt, 2013).

3. The simple rules concept

In today's intricate business landscape, swift decision-making and regular adaptations to evolving circumstances are often crucial (Sull & Eisenhardt, 2012a). To navigate this, some experts suggest that prosperous firms should lean on simple rules rather than intricate strategies (Sull & Eisenhardt, 2012b). While the application of these simple rules might differ based on the organization and context, they generally shine in complex and time-pressured scenarios. They can be seen as cognitive tactics that expedite decisions by streamlining the process (Eisenhardt, 2015; Bingham & Eisenhardt, 2011). This article will further delve into the origins of simple rules, their characteristics, and the keys to their effective application.

3.1. How simple rules are approached

Simple rules address select pivotal challenges within an organization, rather than encompassing every conceivable problem (Sull et al., 2012a). Contrasting with the usage of intricate data and quantitative methods, like the net present value (NPV) assessments, simple rules zero in on a handful of opportunities to achieve objectives (Hutchinson & Gigerenzer, 2005;

Sull et al., 2012a). The literature provides several key steps for formulating simple rules (Eisenhardt & Sull, 2001; Sull & Eisenhardt, 2012a, 2012b, 2015; Eisenhardt, 2015; Maltoni, 2015):

1. Definition of objectives: be as precise and specific as possible.
2. Specification of a mission-critical department or process where opportunities are significant and the resources currently inadequate in order to achieve the overall objectives.
3. Capturing of these opportunities and identification of a few critical issues or areas where simple rules will have the greatest impact.

Sull and Eisenhardt (2012a, 2012b) outline the initial steps for pinpointing the primary bottlenecks. These bottlenecks refer to particular activities or decisions where simple rules can yield the most significant value-enhancing impact (Sull & Eisenhardt, 2015). The subsequent three steps focus on leveraging these opportunities:

4. Further clarification of the key activities necessary and decisions needed to be taken into account to fulfill the mission-critical process or solve the found issues.
5. Discovery of opportunities and their qualification. Use of past experiences and events, as well as heuristics to evaluate what worked and what did not.
6. Definition of a *rule of thumb* for each critical issue. Use of diverse sources and involvement of employees to make creative proposals. Use simple rules to frame exactly how and what is done.

Shared creativity and insights are essential for crafting and effectively enforcing rules. The method for implementing simple rules centers on clearly pinpointing a bottleneck, followed by creating heuristics to address it. Cross-functional teams should participate in shaping these heuristics, tapping into collective creativity. Employees confronted with decision-making challenges are best positioned to formulate them. Concurrently, managers should assign teams and sift through the proposed ideas. To gain a deeper understanding of the simple rules concept, illustrations from the lead authors are provided below.

3.2. What simple rules look like

Scholars suggest simple rules as straightforward guidelines targeting particular organizational tasks, aiming to quickly, clearly, and effectively capture opportunities. As first outlined by Eisenhardt and Sull (2001) and further elaborated in Sull and Eisenhardt (2012a, 2015), there are five types of simple rules guidelines:

- *How-to-Rules* focus on the way of achieving targets. After a critical bottleneck is defined, how-to-rules act as straightforward guidelines, which a team can follow. For example, how-to-rules are used to optimize processes.

- *Boundary Rules* focus on the decision-making process—whether something works with the resources present, or an alternative needs to be reconsidered. Boundary rules are especially important when it comes to innovations and new market developments.

- *Priority Rules* consider the structure of the implementation. Often, companies face a lot of obstacles and need to rank decisions according to the importance of opportunities.

- *Timing Rules*, on the other hand, focus on the implementation schedule. Different opportunities require different timing and times of the year.

- *Exit Rules* define the point of withdrawal during the pursuit of an opportunity, when, at times, a strategy does not work properly. If that point is reached, it is better to focus on the next priority.

A hands-on illustration and breakdown of the five guiding rules, their basic purposes, and example cases illustrating their application can be found in the subsequent table, as detailed by Eisenhardt & Sull (2001):

Type	Purpose	Example Case using Simple Rules
How-To Rules	Focus on key features of the execution of a process. What makes it unique, how can its value be maximized?	**All Logistica** Objective: Cut costs Bottleneck: Capital budgeting Rules of thumb: • Remove obstacles to growing revenues • Minimize up-front expenditure • Provide benefits immediately (rather than paying off in the long term) • Reuse existing resources
Boundary Rules	Decide which opportunities can be pursued and which are not implementable for the organization.	**Lego** Objective: Enter new markets Bottleneck: Integrate the Lego philosophy Rules of thumb: • Products have the Lego look • Children will learn while having fun • Parents will approve of the product • Products maintain high quality standards The product stimulates creativity
Priority Rules	Structure and rank the pursuable opportunities. What should be executed first? What follows?	**Intel** Objective: Prioritize capacity spending Bottleneck: Products Rule of thumb: • Manufacturing capacity allocation is based on the product's gross margin
Timing Rules	Synchronize emerging opportunities with the creation and execution of a strategy. Align all involved parts of the company.	**Nortel Networks** Objective: Perfect old markets and enter new markets Bottleneck: Product Innovation Process Rules of thumb: • Project teams must know the exact time of delivery of products to the most important customers • Development innovation time must be shorter than 18 months
Exit Rules	Decide, when an opportunity cannot be exploited and the company should withdraw.	**Petrochemical Company (anonymous)** Objective: Profit improvement through new catalyst technology Bottleneck: Technology testing Rules of thumb: • Sell of form alliance with partner with superior knowledge if technology fails • Technology testing time limited to 15 months

Table: Description and examples of corporate simple rules (adapted from Eisenhardt & Sull, 2001, Sull & Eisenhardt, 2012b, & Courtney, 2001).

3.3. Applying simple rules successfully

The primary strength of simple rules lies in their role as clear-cut guidelines, which curtail complexity and prevent organizations from being paralyzed by an excess of options. Real-world cases demonstrate that when simple rules are properly implemented, they can optimize processes and even rescue a company from bankruptcy. However, simple rules must be tailored to both the business and the industry, and they should be routinely adjusted to evolving conditions (Sull & Eisenhardt, 2012a). Over time, some rules may lose their relevance and are supplanted by newer ones stemming from enriched understanding and experience (Eisenhardt, 2013; Sull & Eisenhardt, 2012a). Since simple rules often influence multiple departments, transparency becomes crucial. Proposals and decisions should be communicated across different organizational sections to maximize their impact and minimize the risk of unwanted outcomes (Sull & Eisenhardt, 2012a; Eisenhardt, 2015). Sull and Eisenhardt (2015) assert that the efficacy of these rules hinges on four conditions:

- The amount or rules of thumb must be limited,
- The rules need to be adjusted for each organization,
- Issues and possible activities should be clearly defined and stated,
- And the organization should encourage creative impact.

The enduring success of simple rules is contingent upon managers regularly evaluating and modifying them in response to evolving circumstances (Davis et al., 2007; Sull & Eisenhardt, 2012a). Sull and his colleagues (2012a) advocate for routine assessments to ascertain the continued relevance of a rule. These heuristics, born from experience, craft flexible strategies for capitalizing on opportunities. By simplifying cognitive processes, heuristics enhance the innate knowledge of managers. Yet, the efficacy of simple rules is greatly influenced by a company's human resources. Teams with diverse age and experience profiles, which have collaborated frequently in the past, may more effectively harness their collective experience to forge simple rules. The triumph of simple rules is also tethered to the organizational culture and hierarchy. This approach thrives when the corporate ethos empowers staff to devise rules pertinent to their roles and execute them in a timely fashion. It is imperative for managers to place trust in their teams, granting them the autonomy to innovate and express creativity.

4. Concluding thoughts

The concept of simple rules has been around for over two decades, but it still presents an untapped area of study. Though its main proponents, Eisenhardt and Sull, have honed the idea, many case studies highlighting its benefits fall short in explaining how these rules are derived and their long-term effectiveness. Several pressing questions loom: Is simple rules primarily strategic, aimed at addressing overarching business objectives, or is it more of a tactic to deal with day-to-day operational challenges, especially since it emphasizes resolving bottlenecks and practical problem-solving? When companies embrace the simple rules approach, what elements of the traditional strategic planning process does it take over, and which facets remain critical to craft a holistic business strategy? How does simple rules mesh with other prevailing strategic approaches and tools? And for those that dovetail nicely, how can they be smoothly integrated with simple rules? Furthermore, with the current uptick in the availability of data and analytics prowess, and the increasing ability to incorporate real-time data into strategic planning, where does simple rules stand in this data-centric era? Tackling these questions would not only enrich our academic understanding of the simple rules framework but also enhance its practical application in the business world.

References

Andersson, P., Edman, J., & Ekman, M. (2005). Predicting the World Cup 2002 in soccer: Performance and confidence of experts and non-experts. *International Journal of Forecasting, 21*(3), 565-576.

Argote, L. (1999). *Organizational learning: Creating, retaining, and transferring knowledge.* Boston: Kluwer Academic Publishers.

Baker, T., & Nelson, R. E. (2005). Creating something from nothing: Resource construction through entrepreneurial bricolage. *Administrative Science Quarterly, 50*(3), 329-366.

Bingham C. B. (2009). Oscillating improvisation: how entrepreneurial firms create success in foreign market entries over time. *Strategic Entrepreneurship Journal, 3*(4), 321-345.

Bingham, C. B., & Eisenhardt, K. M. (2011). Rational heuristics: The 'simple rules' that strategists learn from process experience. *Strategic Management Journal, 32*(13), 1437-1464.

Bingham, C. B., Eisenhardt, K. M., & Furr, N. R. (2007). What makes a process a capability? Heuristics, strategy, and effective capture of opportunities. *Strategic Entrepreneurship Journal, 1*(1-2), 27-47.

Brown S. L, & Eisenhardt K. M. (1997). The art of continuous change: Linking complexity theoryand time-paced evolution in relentlessly shifting organizations. *Administrative Science Quarterly, 42*(1), 1-34.

Brown S. L., & Eisenhardt K. M. (1998). *Competing on the Edge: Strategy as Structured Chaos.* Boston: Harvard Business School Press.

Bourgeois, L. J., & Eisenhardt, K. M. (1988). Strategic decision processes in high velocity environments: Four case in the microcomputer industry. *Management Science, 34*(7), 816-835.

Courtney, H. (2001). *Crafting strategy in an uncertain world.* Boston: Harvard Business School Press.

Davis, J. P., Eisenhardt K. M., & Bingham C. B. (2007). Developing theory through simulation methods. *Academy of Management Review, 32*(2), 480-499.

Davis, J.P., Eisenhardt K. M., & Bingham C. B. (2009). Optimal structure, market dynamism, and the strategy of simple rules, *Administrative Science Quarterly, 54*(3), 413-452.

Edmondson A. C., Bohmer R. M., & Pisano G. P. (2001). Disrupted routines: Team learning and new technology implementation in hospitals. *Administrative Science Quarterly, 46*(4), 685-716.

Eisenhardt, K. M. (1989). Making fast strategic decisions in high-velocity environments. *TheAcademy of Management Journal, 32*(3), 543-576.

Eisenhardt, K. M. (1990). Speed and strategic choice: How managers accelerate decision-making. *California Management Review, 32*(3), 39-54.

Eisenhardt, K. M. (2013). Top management teams and the performance of entrepreneurial firms. *Small Business Economics, 40*(4), 805-816.

Eisenhardt, K. M. (2015). Kathleen Eisenhardt: Simple Rules for a Complex World [Entire Talk], May 1. Retrieved May 15, 2016, from https://www.youtube.com/watch?v=c- pujS_7OHM

Eisenhardt, K. M. (2015). Simple Rules: How to Thrive in a Complex World, November 3. Retrieved May 15, 2016, from https://www.youtube.com/watch?v=eA0zNA2GiXw

Eisenhardt, K. M., & Bourgeois III, L. J. (1988). Politics of strategic decision-making: Toward a mid-range theory. *Academy of Management Journal, 31*(4), 737-770.

Eisenhardt, K. M., Kahwajy, J. L., & Bourgeois III, L. J. (1997). Conflict and strategic choice:How top management teams disagree. *California Management Review, 39*(2), 42-62.

Eisenhardt, K. M., and Martin J. A. (2000). Dynamic capabilities: What are they? *Strategic Management Journal, 21*(10-11), 1105-1121.

Eisenhardt, K. M., & Sull, D. N. (2001). Strategy as simple rules. *Harvard Business Review, 79*(1), 106-119.

Eisenhardt, K. M., & Zbaracki, M. A. (1992). Strategic decision making. *Strategic Management Journal, 13*(2), 17-37.

Ellonen, H. K., Tuomi, A., & Johansson, A. (2021). Simple rules and learning: Business model innovation during Covid-19. *Proceedings of the ISPIM Connects" Reconnect, Rediscover, Reimagine"*.

Fredrickson, J., & Mitchell, T. (1984). Strategic decision processes: Comprehensiveness and performance in an industry with an unstable environment. *Academy of Management Journal, 27*(2), 399-423.

Gigerenzer, G., Todd, P. M., & The ABC Research Group. (1999). *Simple heuristics that make ussmart*. New York: Oxford University Press.

Goby, V. P., & Karimova, G. Z. (2021). "Simple rules" as an approach to corporate selection of CSR strategies. *International Journal of Organizational Analysis*.

Graebner M. E. (2004). Momentum and serendipity: How acquired leaders create value in the integration of technology firms. *Strategic Management Journal, 25*(8-9), 751-777.

Hallen, B. M. (2008). The causes and consequences of the initial network positions of new organizations: From whom do entrepreneurs receive investments? *Administrative Science Quarterly, 53*(4), 685-718.

Hargadon, A., & Sutton R. I. (1997). Technology brokering and innovation in a product development firm. *Administrative Science Quarterly, 42*(3), 716-749.

Hatch, M. J. (1998). Jazz as a metaphor for organizing in the 21st century. *Organization Science, 9*(5), 556-557.

Hoang, H., & Rothaermel, F. T. (2005). The effect of general and partner-specific alliance experience on joint R&D project performance. *Academy of Management Journal, 48*(2), 332-345.

Hutchinson, H. M. C., & Gigerenzer, G. (2005). Simple heuristics and rules of thumb: Where psychologists and behavioural biologists might meet. *Behavioural Processes, 69*(2), 97-124.

Isen, A. M., Daubman, K. A., & Nowicki, G. P. (1987). Positive affect facilitates creative problem solving. *Journal of Personality and Social Psychology, 52*(6), 1122-1131.

Iyengar, S. S., Huberman, G., & Jiang, W. (2004). How much choice is too much: Determinantsof individual contributions in 401K retirement plans. In: O.S. Mitchell, S. Utkus (Eds.), *Pension Design and Structure: New Lessons from Behavioral Finance*. Oxford: Oxford University Press.

Iyengar, S. S., & Kamenica, E. (2010). Choice proliferation, simplicity seeking, and asset allocation. *Journal of Public Economics, 94*(7-8), 530-539.

Kamenica, E. (2008). Contextual inference in markets: On the informational content of product lines. *American Economic Review, 98*(5), 2127-2149.

Kinni, T. (2015, April 14). Conquering complexity with simple rules. Retrieved May 16, 2016, *from https://www.gsb.stanford.edu/insights/conquering-complexity-simple-rules*

Lahno, B. (2007). Rational choice and rule following behavior. *Rationality and Society, 19*(4), 425-450.

Makridakis, S., & Hibon, M. (1979). Accuracy of forecasting: An empirical investigation. *Journal of the Royal Statistical Society, 142*(2), 97-145.

Makridakis, S., & Hibon, M. (2000). The M3-competition: Results, conclusions and implications. *International Journal of Forecasting, 16*(4), 451-476.

Maltoni, V. (2015, October 06). *For simple rules that Work, Identify the Bottleneck.* Retrieved May 16, 2016, from http://www.conversationagent.com/2015/10/identify-the- bottleneck.html

March, J., & Olsen, J. (1976). *Ambiguity and choice in organizations.* Bergen: Universitetsforlaget.

Martin, J. A., & Eisenhardt K. M. (2010). Rewiring: Cross-business-unit collaborations and performance in multi-business organizations. *Academy of Management Journal, 53*(2), 265-301.

Miller, D., & Friesen P. H. (1980). Momentum and revolution in organizational adaptation. *Academy of Management Journal, 23*(4), 591-614.

Miner, A. S., Bassoff, P., & Moorman, C. (2001). Organizational improvisation and learning: Afield study. *Administrative Science Quarterly, 46*(2), 304-337.

Mintzberg, H., Raisinghani, D., & Theoret, A. (1976). The structure of "unstructured" decisionprocesses. *Administrative Science Quarterly, 21*(2), 246-275.
Newell, A., & Simon, H.A. (1972). *Human problem solving.* Englewood Cliffs: Prentice-Hall.

Okhuysen, G. A., & Eisenhardt, K. M. (2002). Integrating knowledge in groups: How formal interventions enable flexibility. *Organization Science, 13*(4), 370-386.

Owen-Smith, J., & Powell W. W. (2003). Knowledge networks as channels and conduits: The effects of spillovers in the Boston biotechnology community. *Organization Science, 15*(1), 5-21.

Pisano, G. P. (1994). Knowledge, integration, and the locus of learning: An empirical analysis ofprocess development. *Strategic Management Journal, 15*(1), 85-100.

Rieskamp, J., & Otto, P. E. (2006). SSL: A theory of how people learn to select strategies. *Journal of Experimental Psychology, 135*(2), 207-236.

Roberts, P. W. (1999). Product innovation, product-market competition, and persistent profitability in the U.S. pharmaceutical industry. *Strategic Management Journal, 20*(7), 655-670.

Rindova, V., & Kotha, S. (2001). Continuous morphing: Competing through dynamic capabilities, form, and function. *Academy of Management Journal, 44*(6), 1263-1280.

Rothaermel, F. T., Hitt, M., & Jobe, L. (2006). Balancing vertical integration and strategic outsourcing: Effects on product portfolios, new product success, and firm performance. *Strategic Management Journal, 27*(11), 1033-1056.

Rowley, T. J., Behrens, D. & Krackhardt, D. (2000). Redundant governance structures: An analysis of structural and relational embeddedness in the steel and semiconductor industries. *Strategic Management Journal, 21*(3), 369-386.

Schweiger, D., Sandberg, W., & Ragan, J. (1986). Group approaches for improving strategic decision making: A comparative analysis of dialectical inquiry, devil's advocacy, and consensus. *Academy of Management Journal, 29*(1), 51-71.

Scheibehenne, B., & Bröder, A. (2007). Predicting Wimbledon 2005 tennis results by mere player name recognition. *Journal of Forecasting, 23*(3), 415-426.

Siggelkow, N. (2001). Change in the presence of fit: The rise, the fall, and the renaissance of LizClaiborne. *Academy of Management Journal, 44*(4), 838-857.

Simon H. A. (1973). The structure of ill-structured problems. *Artificial Intelligence, 4*(3-4), 181-202.

Sapienza H. J., Autio E., George, G, & Zahra S. A. (2006). A capabilities perspective on the effects of early internationalization on firm survival and growth. *Academy of Management Review, 31*(4), 914-933.

Staw, B., Sandelands, L., & Dutton, J. (1981). Threat-rigidity effects in organizational behavior: A multilevel analysis. *Administrative Science Quarterly, 26*(4), 501-524.

Sull, D., & Eisenhardt, K. M. (2012a). Simple rules for a complex world. *Harvard Business Review, 90*(9), 69-76.

Sull, D., & Eisenhardt, K. M. (2012b). Shape strategy with simple rules, not complex frameworks. September 27. *Retrieved May 16, 2016 from https://hbr.org/2012/09/shape-strategy-with-simple-rules.*

Sull, D., & Eisenhardt, K. M. (2015). *Simple rules: How to thrive in a complex world.* Boston: Houghton Mifflin Harcourt.

Sun, S. L., Xiao, J., Zhang, Y., & Zhao, X. (2018). Building business models through simple rules. *Multinational Business Review.*

Teece, D. J., Pisano, G., & Shuen, A. (1997). Dynamic capabilities and strategic management. *Strategic Management Journal, 18*(7), 509-533.

Vroom, V., & Yetton, P. (1973). *Leadership and decision making.* Pittsburgh: University of Pittsburgh Press.

Vermeulen F., Barkema H. G. (2001). Learning through acquisitions. *Academy of ManagementJournal, 44*(3), 457-476.

Weick, K. E. (1979). *The social psychology of organizing (2d. ed.).* Reading: Addison-Wesley. Weick, K.E. (1998). Improvisation as a mindset. *Organization Science, 9*(5), 543-555.

Weick. K. E. (1993). The collapse of sensemaking in organizations: The Mann Gulch disaster. *Administrative Science Quarterly, 38*(4), 628-652.

Wiggins, R. R., & Ruefli, T. P. (2005). Schumpeter's ghost: Is hypercompetition making the best of times shorter? *Strategic Management Journal, 26*(10), 887-911.

Part III:
Further Topics in Behavioral Strategy

Emotions in Strategy

Marcel Hermle, Robert LoBue, Yasmin Richwien and
Daniel Simonovich

Abstract. This literature review focuses on the role of emotions in behavioral strategy research. Emotions arise from various appraisals and can be viewed from different perspectives, from individual to interpersonal, group, and organizational levels. The relationship between emotions and strategy is crucial because strategic shifts can evoke emotions that impact the success of strategy implementation. While the significance of emotions in the workplace has often been overlooked in past strategy discussions, recent research has started exploring innovative concepts, such as emotional aperture, to understand the interplay between emotions and strategy. This includes considerations of hierarchy levels, leadership styles, company size, and global contexts.

Keywords: behavioral strategy, individual emotions, collective and group-focus emotions, multi-level framework of emotions, radical change, strategic renewal, emotional aperture.

1. Introduction

Behavioral strategy aims to blend social and cognitive psychology with strategic management theories and practices (Powell et al., 2011). This research domain seeks to integrate theories of human thought, social actions, and emotions into the strategic management of organizations. As a result, it expands both empirical studies and strategy theories, drawing out practical implications for real-world strategic management. One area of psychology that hasn't been widely integrated into strategy research is human emotion. However, inspired by advancements in neuroscience and social psychology, and spurred by early work from researchers like Huy (1999, 2002, 2005), the past two decades have seen a growing interest in connecting micro psychological phenomena to strategic outcomes (Hodgkinson & Healey, 2011; Huy, 2011; Powell et al., 2011). Additionally, the idea of emotion-based capabilities has been framed within the theoretical construct of emotional intelligence (Salovey & Mayer, 1990 and 1997).

This has led to a substantial body of literature that examines the impact of emotions on individual cognition and behavior. Given that the central question of strategy research revolves around factors influencing organizational performance, behavioral strategy research also delves into collective emotions and underscores their significance in executing strategies successfully. For instance, Higgs and Dulewicz (2002) view the formation of strategic outcomes not just as a logical process but also place equal emphasis on the role of emotional processes, as depicted in Figure 1.

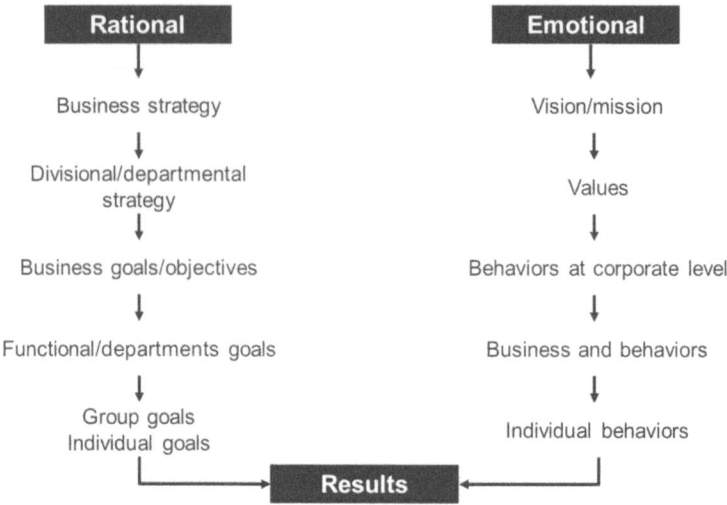

Figure 1: Rational and emotional aspects of strategy (Higgs & Dulewicz, 2002).

In contemporary academic discussions, there's a growing recognition of the significance of emotions as subjective elements in strategic considerations, shifting the focus away from only objective factors. This literature review pinpoints this area as an emerging segment of behavioral strategy. The review zeroes in on how emotions, originating at the individual level, influence organizational outcomes and delves into particular organizational situations where emotions could potentially influence strategic decision-making.

2. Emotions

Emotions significantly impact human behavior and cognition, especially during situations riddled with uncertainty and ambiguity. Consequently, they play a vital role in decision-making, strategic reasoning, and outcomes (Elfenbein, 2007). While emotions encompass a broad research area, a definition from Sanchez-Burks and Huy (2009) offers a foundational perspective: "Emotions involve a combination of psychological and biological reactions, stemming from an assessment of a particular situation or entity. They often manifest as personal experiences and distinct behavioral responses."

Historically, terms such as emotion, affect, and mood were often used interchangeably. However, contemporary research encourages clearer distinctions. Russell & Feldman Barrett (2009, p. 104) define affect as "a basic, non-reflective feeling apparent in moods and emotions, always within one's conscious grasp." Affect might exist independently or alongside emotion and mood. On the other hand, moods are broader feelings, not directly tied to a specific source, and generally last longer than emotions and affects (Frijda, 2009).

People express emotional signals both verbally and non-verbally, using facial expressions and gestures (Ekman and Friesen 1974; Rosenthal et al., 1979). Their display often varies based on the social context (Elfenbein, 2007). Through "emotional regulation," emotions can be subdued or adjusted post-assessment (Gross, 1998). With appropriate regulation, emotions can effectively steer focus to relevant topics (Gross, 1998). Academic works often classify emotions into positive (e.g. hope, pride, gratitude) and negative (e.g. fear, anger, frustration) groups. These emotions can arise from real events or simply the anticipation of change (Frijda, 1988). For a deeper dive into emotions within the realm of strategy, upcoming sections explore how specific emotions are linked to particular triggers and how they manifest across organizational levels.

2.1. Specific emotions

According to the theory of emotional appraisal, certain emotions, including fear and hope, are linked to appraisals. These appraisals are unique combinations of specific behavioral dimensions, such as certainty and the ability to control a situation (Smith & Ellsworth, 1985; Smith, 1989). While both fear and anger are negative emotions that evoke unpleasant feelings, they stem from different origins and lead to distinct outcomes. Fear arises from feeling out of control and facing high uncertainty, typically leading to the desire to escape (Roseman, 1991; Tiedens & Linton, 2001). On the other hand, anger is tied to a sense of certainty about a situation (Roseman, 1991; Tiedens & Linton, 2001), pushing one towards seeking revenge (Frijda, 1988) and confrontation (Folkman & Lazarus, 1988). At its core, this theory suggests that basic emotions can be pinpointed by the relationship between their specific triggers and the ensuing emotional responses. To truly grasp the nuances of emotions, it is crucial to consider the interpersonal elements of emotion, whether it is concerning an individual or between members of a group, as discussed in the subsequent section.

2.2. Multi-level framework of emotions

According to Ashkanasy's (2003) multi-layered model of emotions in organizations, emotions manifest at five distinct levels within businesses. These levels are categorized into four categories, as illustrated in Figure 2.

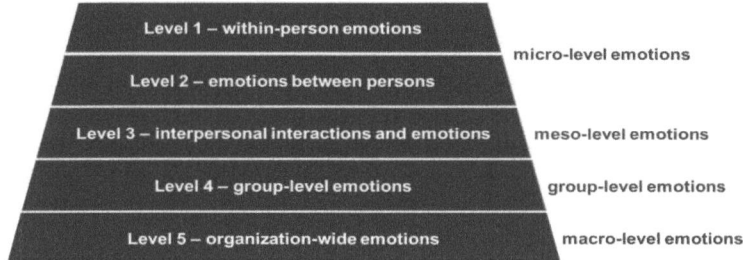

Figure 2:   Multi-level framework of emotions (Ashkanasy, 2007).

The first two levels of the framework are combined into one category, while the subsequent three levels each correspond directly to their own unique categories. These distinctions are further elaborated upon in the sections that follow.

2.2.1. Micro-level emotions

The initial category of the framework, micro-level emotions, focuses on individual behavioral reactions stemming from personal experiences, whether internal or through interactions with others. Research on Level 1 within-person emotions of Ashkenasy's model (Weiss & Cropanzano, 1996; To et al., 2012) indicates that an individual's emotions can fluctuate constantly, shifting from moment to moment. Emotions are typically viewed as internal experiences, connected to personal issues, such as individual goals, resources, and concerns. This perspective implies that individual emotions are dynamic, profoundly influencing personal behaviors and actions. These emotions play a significant role in strategic decision-making.

Level 2 of the framework explores emotions between persons, commonly called individual differences. This level looks at specific characteristics of individuals, where inherent emotional tendencies might lean more towards interpersonal positivity or negativity. Past studies have shown that these traits can influence personal outcomes within organizational contexts (Staw & Barsade, 1993; Fox & Spector, 2000), encompassing the strategic operations of companies.

2.2.2. Meso-level emotions

The second category in Ashkenasy's framework is meso-level emotions, which includes Level 3, focusing on interpersonal interactions and the transmission of emotions (Rousseau, 1985). Clore (1994) highlights that emotions play a crucial role in communication, emphasizing the significance of certain messages. Additionally, emotions conveyed non-verbally, like through voice tone, facial expressions, and body language, underscore the message's importance (Ekman, 1982). As a result, the communicative aspect of emotions is vital for organizational managers to consider when formulating and conveying strategic plans (Ashkanasy, 2003). Furthermore, Ashkanasy (2003) believes that meso-level emotions serve as a pivotal bridge, connecting micro-level emotions to those in the third category, group-level emotions of Level 4, and extending to the fourth category, macro-level emotions, which are organization-wide emotions of Level 5.

2.2.3. Group-level emotions

The third category, group-level emotions, is positioned at the fourth level of the model. Groups are described as "collections of two or more individuals who consistently collaborate to attain shared goals" (Schermerhorn et al., 2001, p. 174). While group collaboration typically offers benefits, it can also heighten the intricacies of emotions and relationships, given the multiple individuals involved, each with distinct emotional responses. For instance, during a waste facility construction project, Welcomer et al. (2000) noted that stakeholders' emotions, including both project developers and local residents, significantly impacted communication. The predominant negative emotional responses from residents conflicted with the logical arguments of the developers, impairing effective communication. Hence, corporate strategists must engage with stakeholders transparently and productively to assist in ensuring emotions don't hinder strategic goals.

"Collective emotions are the amalgamation of the group members' shared emotional responses" (Barsade & Gibson, 1998). Such emotions can influence a group uniformly—with every member experiencing similar feelings—or diversely, where some might have positive feelings while others have negative reactions to the same event. Emotions can also ripple across members, leading to mutual feelings within groups (Barsade & Gibson, 1998). Organizationally, since employees have varied responses to strategic decisions based on personal impacts, their emotional reactions to corporate strategies can differ broadly (Cyert & March, 1992).

According to emotion appraisal theories (Smith & Ellsworth, 1985; Ellsworth & Scherer, 2003), emotions surface when individuals deem events as either favorable or detrimental to their objectives. However, emotions can also arise when significant events impact others they care about, even if they are not directly affected. For instance, group-level emotions can manifest when fans feel joy over their football team's victory (Smith et al., 2007). Milgram (1992) posits that people are more inclined to act if they perceive others' emotions as mirroring their own.

Moreover, emotions focused on the group are strongly tied to social identity (Dutton & Dukerich, 1991). Social identities, stemming from shared backgrounds or languages, can evoke such emotions in managers, prompting them to either endorse or reject particular strategic alternatives, even if they are not directly impacted (Huy, 2011). These insights suggest that managers might make strategic choices that cater to group members with shared social identities, given the intertwined nature of group-centric emotions.

2.2.4. Macro-level emotions

The fourth and concluding category of Ashkenasy's model encompasses macro-level emotions, specifically Level 5 organization-wide emotions. These macro-level emotions are more subtle and can be more challenging to discern compared to emotions on the preceding levels. It is vital to evaluate and grasp the emotional climate of an entire organization. de Rivera defines this as "an objective group phenomenon that can be felt—much like the ambiance of a party or city, exuding joy or melancholy, openness or apprehension" (1992, p. 197). Yet, it is crucial to distinguish the emotional climate from corporate culture. The latter is characterized more by a consistent set of values, standards, and beliefs rather than being purely emotional (Ashkanasy et al., 2000; Ashkanasy, 2003). Unlike the extensive literature on individual emotions, the study of organization-wide emotions is a relatively newer but rapidly growing field (Campbell et al., 2003; Madlock, 2008; Voronov & Vince, 2012). This emerging area presents ample exploration opportunities for scholars.

2.3. Recognizing emotions in strategy

The concept of emotion spans a wide research domain, covering multiple organizational levels and relating to various behavioral affective states. Given that strategy inherently encompasses overarching organizational and behavioral impacts, it is essential to define a clear framework for emotions in strategy. Creating such a framework not only provides a foundation for future research but also offers practical implications. This structure will facilitate the ongoing inclusion of new research findings into a holistic system dedicated to the study of emotions in strategic decision-making.

3. Emotions in strategy context

Strategy, as a vast research domain, emphasizes the strategic events that provoke specific emotions, as postulated in behavioral strategy studies. Broadly speaking, strategy is the blueprint devised to achieve long-term goals or competitive advantages for an organization (Chandler, 1963; Porter, 1996). Research suggests that individuals experience emotions when they perceive events as affecting their wellbeing or objectives. These emotions subsequently influence their thought processes and actions (Ellsworth & Smith, 1988; Lazarus, 1991). As a result, in strategic contexts, emotions can significantly shape a company's strategy implementation and, ultimately, its overall competitive position.

3.1. Radical change

A primary strategic scenario for an organization, capable of triggering collective emotions among large groups of employees, is radical change (Huy, 2012; Bartunek, 1984). Such change is often related to strategic actions including mergers, acquisitions (Kusstatscher & Cooper, 2005), shifts in organizational identity (Corley & Gioia, 2004), downsizing efforts, divestitures, and the formation of strategic alliances or joint ventures (Noer, 1993; Fox & Amichai-Hamburger, 2001). Since radical change typically introduces uncertainty, it is vital to understand that uncertainty often leads to fear as a primal emotional response.

3.2. Strategic renewal

Another organizational process with strategic relevance that can incite collective emotions is strategic renewal (Huy, 2009). While strategic renewal is an evolutionary process that unfolds over extended periods, radical change is typically more abrupt and revolutionary (Weick & Quinn, 1999).

Even so, teams tasked with guiding the organization's strategic renewal often operate in high-pressure, emotionally charged settings. This emotional backdrop can influence their decision-making, actions, and eventual results (Brown & Eisenhardt, 1997; Floyd & Lane, 2000). Moreover, as noted by Kanter (1983) and Fineman (2003), employees' emotional responses to a company's new strategic direction can amplify when confronted with changing and disputed ideas.

From a research perspective, strategic renewal can be segmented into three distinct organizational processes (Huff et al., 1992; Floyd & Lane, 2000):

- *Competence Modification*: Recognizing the need for change and the imperative for a new strategic direction.
- *Competence Definition*: Assessing and determining the company's capabilities and exploring potential alternatives.
- *Competence Deployment*: Implementing the strategy post-decision.

As these strategic processes unfold, individual employees and teams will likely process and respond to them emotionally, influenced by their perceptions and assessments. Floyd and Lane (2000) associated individual emotional responses with these processes. Additionally, Huy (2009) suggested "team emotional tone" should be recognized in strategic contexts, very similar to the concept of "group affective tone" (George, 1995). This tone is intimately connected to prevailing moods. Huy also proposed that while appraisals can spark emotions, the reverse is equally possible: emotions can lead to cognitive appraisals. Huy's model in his article "Interaction between Cognition and Emotion in Strategic Renewal Processes" illustrates how certain appraisals and emotional tones influence specific organizational activities at a collective level. For instance, an emotional tone rooted in hope, paired with expectations of future success and adequate capability, enhances competence deployment (Huy, 2009).

3.3 Anticipating appraisals and resulting emotions in strategy

Situations involving strategic change and renewal are frequently charged with emotions. Specific perceptions, such as the level of certainty or control over a situation, can provoke intense emotional reactions. White et. al. (2022) of EY and Oxford University conclude from their in-depth analysis of a survey with over 2000 respondents from 23 countries across seven industries that leaders of transformation must seek "to mitigate emotional harm to - and drive emotional commitment from - employees." For effective emotion management in strategic contexts, it is crucial to anticipate these emotional responses and address them based on their anticipated assessment.

4. Emotion in practical application

In the past, expressing emotions in the workplace was not common in Western cultures. Sanchez-Burks (2005) believes this practice stemmed from the Protestant and Calvinist work ethic, emphasizing task-oriented behaviors. As a result, individuals often overlooked emotional cues in professional settings. Tichy and Sherman (1994) note that many organizations, uncertain about handling emotions, chose to ignore them altogether. However, it is essential for businesses to recognize the significance of emotions, especially collective ones. Positive group emotions, for instance, have been associated with improved customer service and decreased absenteeism (George, 1995). On the other hand, negative group emotions can adversely impact overall team performance (Duffy & Shaw, 2000).

Gross (1998) sees "emotional regulation," the balance between reason and emotion, as crucial. This balance allows managers to maintain focus and prioritize where to allocate resources and time. Subsequent sections will delve into practical applications and strategies for effectively managing emotions in organizational contexts.

4.1. Emotion perception

Strategic events often spark emotions in groups, both large and small. Changes in strategy, in particular, can stir collective emotions (Huy, 2012). Managers should not overlook the influence of these emotions at an organizational level.

In settings such as start-ups, even small teams have a profound impact on the company's long-term success. Launching a business is typically fraught with uncertainty but is pivotal for the future well-being of both founders and investors. As such, their emotions can significantly shape their actions and entrepreneurial mindset (Baron, 2008; Cardon et al., 2009). Start-up leaders must be proactive in managing their emotions, as they can sway crucial strategic decisions either negatively or positively.

In essence, it is vital for all managers, whether in massive corporations or fledgling start-ups, to recognize the potential emotions that might arise among employees. With this understanding, they can predict how these emotions might impact performance and then strategize how best to manage them, ultimately aiming to boost shareholder value.

4.2. Emotional aperture

In times of strategic change, leaders must effectively navigate emotions by employing emotional aperture, a skill that enables them to discern the mix of emotions within a group (Sanchez-Burks & Huy, 2009). Several research findings offer insights for leaders aiming to harness this ability:

- Positive emotions are generally easier to identify than negative ones (Elfenbein and Ambady, 2002).

- Leaders with a keen sense of emotional recognition are often seen as transformational by their teams (Bass, 1999; Rubin et al., 2005) and are better equipped to oversee change (Sanchez-Burks & Huy, 2009).

- Group emotions are fluid, so leaders should dynamically adjust their emotional aperture to respond accordingly (Sanchez-Burks & Huy, 2009).

For instance, during organizational change, there might be distinct emotional responses in different subgroups. A majority might feel fear, potentially impeding strategy implementation, while a minority might be optimistic and hopeful. By harnessing emotional aperture, leaders can pinpoint these emotions. They can then address the majority's fears by highlighting the optimism and hope from the minority, fostering a more unified approach to change (Huy, 2011; Sanchez-Burks & Huy, 2009).

4.3. Emotional capability

Huy's research in 1999 and 2005 contrasts the concept of individual emotional aperture with organizational emotional capability. The latter pertains to an organization's proficiency in recognizing and monitoring collective emotions. Huy posits that businesses emphasizing emotion management, characterized by practices and training focused on emotional routines, tend to navigate strategic change more effectively. These organizations, fortified by robust emotion management, often don't need to lean heavily on individual emotional intelligence.

In the context of strategic change, Huy outlines several emotion management strategies, including reconciliation, experiencing, encouragement, identification, playfulness, and allowing freedom of expression. One key insight is the role of employees' identification with their organization, especially concerning core values. When these values are potentially disrupted by change, effective emotion management ensures stability, negating the need for sudden alterations to soothe employee anxieties. This stability in core values then enhances the success of the organization's strategic transition.

4.4. Hierarchy levels

Although strategy execution can affect all organizational levels, studies highlight the potential influences of middle managers during change processes (Floyd & Wooldridge, 1992; Huy, 2002; Balogun & Johnson, 2004). The behavior of subordinates could be affected by emotions of their middle managers who hold leadership positions in the organization hierarchy (Sy, Côté, & Saavedra, 2005). Middle managers monitor their subordinates' activities and behaviors directly, whereas top-level managers are advised to observe group-focus emotions of their middle managers in order to be informed and to intervene at an early stage in cases where any undesirable developments emerge (Huy, 2011).

The success of this approach likely depends on the emotional aperture of the executives. As top and middle managers are highly involved and share tasks during change processes, Sanchez-Burks and Huy (2009) recommend that emotional aperture is not limited to a certain hierarchy level. To derive specific practical recommendations for the application of emotional aperture for each organizational level and intergroup relationship, awareness and resolutions for different emotional patterns across the various hierarchy levels and subgroups need to be further analyzed and considered.

4.5. International context

Mergers in an international context can be hindered by factors tied to cultural disparities, as suggested by Stahl & Voigt (2008). Each firm's cultural heritage, forming a part of its social identity, can evoke group-centric emotions among employees, given the known connection between group emotions and social identity. Research by Vaara et al. (2005) and Huy (2011) underscores that languages spoken during times of change can contain emotionally charged symbols, potentially leading to conflicts. Such confrontations can negatively affect the integration process, especially in culturally diverse firms.

Recognizing emotions accurately can be especially challenging in a multicultural backdrop. For instance, East Asian cultures typically process social cues collectively, while Western societies lean towards individual processing (Nisbett et al., 2001). Huy (2011) notes that increased ethnic diversity within a group can diminish the precision of detecting specific group emotions. Nonetheless, proficiency in discerning these collective emotions tends to grow with more exposure to multicultural contexts.

5. Research gaps in terms of emotions in strategy

Despite recent advancements in behavioral strategy research, unaddressed areas persist within the subset of emotions in strategy. These areas can be classified into research gaps that are content-related and process-related. Content-related research gaps pertain to examinations of psychological phenomena vital to expanding the understanding of emotions affecting strategic processes. For instance, while individual emotions have been extensively studied, the adverse effects of collective emotions on strategic outcomes have been under-researched. There is a lack of identification of holistic behavioral patterns for managing these collective emotions within organizational practices, including understanding the development of organizational routines tied to emotional capabilities.

Furthermore, at the leadership levels of organizations, potential research could investigate how individual executives or groups, such as top and middle management, succeed or fail in regulating their emotions, thereby influencing their strategic objectives. Delving deeper into how managers impact their subordinates' emotions can offer insights into emotional capability and leadership. The facets of emotions within an organizational context, affecting key executives in understanding and managing both personal and organizational emotions, also present abundant research opportunities.

In the entrepreneurial sphere, there's a deficit of empirical studies on how emotions influence entrepreneurial actions and the growth trajectory of new enterprises. A limited number of studies explore how founders manage their emotions during the initial phases of their business, raising questions concerning varied emotion regulation strategies and their influence on strategic directions of startups.

Regarding organizational processes, research gaps exist concerning the primary drivers of emotions, their specific organizational effects, and the associated managerial challenges. There is an opportunity to study how sudden versus gradual changes elicit different emotional reactions among various subgroups. By associating specific strategic events with certain emotional outcomes, one could aim to identify a series of emotional triggers. Moreover, the exploration of collective and group-level emotions and their unique impact on strategy implementation is promising. By connecting evaluations and outcomes from their emotional reactions, future research could focus on developing practical strategies to counter any potential negative effects therefrom.

6. Conclusion

Emotions have become an intriguing focus within the realm of behavioral studies, and the challenge lies in how they will be integrated into managerial decisions. Will leaders rely on the hard-to-quantify realm of feelings and emotions, or will they stay tethered to objective, quantifiable data inputs?

Research has illuminated the role emotions play in organizational outcomes. This role is especially pronounced during significant changes such as ownership shifts or organizational overhauls. Such transitions, fraught with uncertainty, can elicit strong negative emotions among employees and stakeholders, which might then impact the success of managerial decisions. Despite the wealth of insights, the academic discourse on the subject is still in its early stages, with several complementary viewpoints but few divergent ones.

On the other hand, industry professionals have historically undervalued the power of emotions, often not possessing the tools or methodologies to address them effectively. Established managerial tools, though valuable, seldom underscore the importance of emotions in their frameworks. As such, there's a growing need for collaboration between scholars and industry professionals to bridge this knowledge gap.

Moreover, in our rapidly globalizing world, where interactions span continents and cultures, understanding and managing emotions becomes even more complex. Leaders must be equipped with tools that heighten their cultural sensitivity, allowing them to navigate the myriad of emotional responses they might encounter. Delving into the emotional intelligence and awareness of organizations seems to be a promising direction, potentially paving the way for more informed and empathetic managerial strategies in the future.

References

Ashkanasy, N. M., Wilderom, C. P. M., & Peterson, M. F. (2000). Introduction. In Ashkanasy, N. M., Wilderom, C. P. M., & Peterson M. F. (Eds.), *Handbook of Organizational Culture & Climate*. Thousand Oaks: Sage Publications, (pp. 1-18).

Ashkanasy, N. M. (2003). Emotions in organizations: A multi-level perspective. In Dansereau, F., & Yammarino, F. J. (Eds.), *Multi-level Issues in Organizational Behavior and Strategy*. Amsterdam: JAI, (pp. 9-54).

Ashkanasy, N. M., & Ashton-James, C. E. (2007). Positive emotion in organizations: A multi-level framework. In Cooper, C. L., & Nelson, D. (Eds.), *Positive Organizational Behavior*. Chichester, UK: John Wiley & Sons, (pp. 57-73).

Balogun J., & Johnson, G. (2004). Organizational restructuring and middle manager sensemaking. *Academy of Management Journal, 47*(4), (pp. 523-549).

Baron, R. A. (2008). The role of affect in the entrepreneurial process. *Academy of Management Review, 33*(2), (pp. 328-340).

Barsade, S. G., & Gibson, D. E. (1998). Group emotion: A view from top and bottom. In Neale, M. A., & Mannix, E. A. (Eds.), *Research on Managing Groups and Teams*. Stamford, CT: JAI Press, (pp. 81-102).

Bass, B. M. (1999). Two decades of research and development in transformational leadership. *European Journal of Work and Organizational Psychology, 8*(1), (pp. 9-32).

Bartunek, J. M. (1984). Changing interpretive schemes and organizational restructuring: The example of a religious order. *Administrative Science Quarterly, 29*(3), (pp. 355-387).

Brown, S., & Eisenhardt, K. (1997). The art of continuous change: Linking complexity theory and time-paced evolution in relentlessly shifting organizations. *Administrative Science Quarterly, 42*(1), (pp. 1-34).

Campbell, K. S., White, C. D., & Johnson, D. E. (2003). Leader-member relations as a function of rapport management. *The Journal of Business Communication, 40*(3), (pp. 170-194).

Cardon, M., Wincent, J., Singh, J., & Drnovsek, M. (2009). The nature and experience of entrepreneurial passion. *The Academy of Management Review (AMR), 34*(3), (pp. 511-532).

Chandler, A.D. (1963). *Strategy and Structure: Chapters in the History of American Enterprise*. Cambridge: MIT Press.

Clore, G. C. (1994). Why emotions are felt. In Ekman, P., & Davidson, R. J. (Eds.), *The Nature of Emotions*. New York: Oxford University Press, (pp. 103-111).

Corley, K. G., & Gioia, D. A. (2004). Identity ambiguity and change in the wake of a corporate spin-off. *Administrative Science Quarterly, 49*(2), (pp. 173-208).

Cyert, R. M., & March, J. G. (1992). *A Behavioral Theory of the Firm*. Blackwell, Cambridge, MA.

de Rivera, J. (1992). Emotional climate: Social structure and emotional dynamics. In *International Review of Studies on Emotion Vol. 2*. John Wiley & Sons, (pp. 197-218).

Duffy, M., & Shaw, J. D. (2000). The Salieri syndrome: Consequences of envy in groups. *Small Group Research, 31*(1), (pp. 3-23).

Dutton, J. E., & Dukerich, J. M. 1991. Keeping an eye on the mirror: Image and identity in organizational adaptation. *Academy of Management Journal, 34*(3), (pp. 517-554).

Ekman, P., & Friesen, W. V. (1974). Detecting deception from body or face. *Journal of Personality and Social Psychology, 29*(3), (pp. 288-298).

Ekman, P. (1982). *Emotion in the Human Face* (2nd ed.). Cambridge: Cambridge University Press.

Elfenbein, H. A., & Ambady, N. (2002). Is there an ingroup advantage in emotion recognition? *Psychological Bulletin, 128*(2), (pp. 243-249).

Elfenbein, H. A. (2007). Emotions in organizations: A review and theoretical integration. *Academy of Management Annals, 1*(1), (pp. 371-457).

Ellsworth, P. C., & Smith, C. A. (1988). Shades of joy: Patterns of appraisal differentiating pleasant emotions. *Cognition and Emotion, 2*(4), (pp. 301-331).

Ellsworth, P. C., & Scherer, K. R. (2003). Appraisal processes in emotion. In Davidson R., Goldsmith H., & Scherer K. R. (Eds.), *Handbook of Affective Sciences*, Oxford University Press: New York, (pp. 572-595).

Fineman, S. (1993). Emotions as organizational arenas? In S. Fineman (Ed.), *Emotions in Organizations*. London, UK: Sage Publications, (pp. 9-35).

Fineman, S. (2000). *Emotion in Organizations* (2nd ed.). London, UK: Sage Publications.

Fineman, S. (2003). *Understanding Emotion at Work*. London, UK: Sage Publications.

Fineman, S. (2003). Emotionalizing organizational learning. In Easterby-Smith, M. & Lyles, M. A. (Eds.), *The Blackwell Handbook of Organizational Learning and Knowledge Management*. Oxford, UK: Blackwell, (pp. 557-574).

Floyd, S. W., & Wooldridge, B. (1992). Middle management involvement in strategy and its association with strategic type: a research note. *Strategic Management Journal, 13*(S1), (pp. 153-167).

Floyd, S.W., & Lane, P. J. (2000). Strategizing throughout the organization: managing role conflict in strategic renewal. *Academy of Management Review, 25*(1), (pp. 154-177).

Folkman, S., & Lazarus, R. S. (1988). Coping as a mediator of emotion. *Journal of Personality and Social Psychology, 54*(3), (pp. 466–475). https://doi.org/10.1037/0022-3514.54.3.466

Fox, S., & Amichai-Hamburger, Y. (2001). The power of emotional appeals in promoting organizational change programs. *Academy of Management Executive, 15*(4), (pp. 84-94).

Fox, S., & Spector, P. E. (2000). Relations of emotional intelligence, practical intelligence, general intelligence, and trait affectivity with interview outcomes: It's not all just "G". *Journal of Organizational Behavior: The International Journal of Industrial, Occupational and Organizational Psychology and Behavior, 21*(2), (pp. 203-220).

Frijda, N. H. (1986). *The Emotions.* Cambridge UK: Cambridge University Press.

Frijda, N. H. (1988). The laws of emotion. *American Psychologist, 43*(5), (pp. 349-358).

Frijda, N. H. (2009), Mood. In Sander, D., & Scherer, K. R. (Eds.), *The Oxford Companion to Emotion and the Affective Sciences.* Oxford University Press, (pp. 258-259).

George, J. M. (1990). Personality, affect, and behaviour in groups. *Journal of Applied Psychology, 75*(2), (pp. 107-116).

George, J. M., & Brief, A. P. (1992). Feeling good—doing good: A conceptual analysis of the mood at work-organizational spontaneity relationship. *Psychology Bulletin, 112*(2), (pp. 310-329).

George, J. M. (1995). Leader positive mood and group performance: The case of customer service, *Journal of Applied Social Psychology, 25*(9), (pp. 778-794).

Gross, J. J. (1998). The emerging field of emotion regulation: An integrative review. *Review of General Psychology, 2*(3), (pp. 271-299).

Higgs, M., & Dulewicz, V. (2002). Making Sense of Emotional Intelligence (2nd ed.). Slough, UK: National Foundation for Educational Research.

Hodgkinson, G. P., & Healey, M. P. (2011). Psychological foundations of dynamic capabilities: Reflexion and reflection in strategic management. *Strategic Management Journal, 32*(13), (pp. 1500-1516).

Huff, J. O., Huff, A. S., & Thomas, H. (1992). Strategic renewal and the interaction of cumulative stress and inertia. *Strategic Management Journal, 13*(S1), (pp. 55-75).

Huy, N. Q. (1999). Emotional capability, emotional intelligence, and radical change. *Academy of Management Review, 24*(2), (pp. 325-345).

Huy, N. Q. (2002). Emotional balancing: The role of middle managers in radical change. *Administrative Science Quarterly, 47*(1), (pp. 31-69).

Huy, N. Q. (2005). An emotion-based view of strategic renewal. In Szulanski, G., Porac, J., & Doz, Y. (Eds.), *Strategy Process (Advances in Strategic Management, Vol. 22).* Leeds, UK: Emerald Group Publishing Limited, (pp. 3-37).

Huy, N. Q. (2009). Interaction between cognition and emotion on processes of strategic renewal. *Academy of Management* [Meeting Abstract], August 1.

Huy, N. Q. (2011). How Collective Emotions and Social Identities Influence Strategy Execution. *INSEAD*, Version 24 March 2011.

Huy, N. Q. (2012). Emotions in Strategic Organization: Opportunities for Impactful Research. *INSEAD*, Working Paper No. 2012/51/ST.

Kanter, R. M. (1983). *The Change Masters*. New York: Simon and Schuster.

Kusstatscher, V., & Cooper, C. L. (2005). *Managing Emotions in Mergers and Acquisitions*. Cheltenham, UK &; Northhampton, MA: Edward Elgar.

Lazarus, R. S. (1991). *Emotion and Adaptation*. New York: Oxford University Press.

Levinthal, D. A. (2011). A behavioral approach to strategy - What's the alternative? *Strategic Management Journal, 32*(13), (pp. 1517-1523).

Mackie, D. M., Devos, T., & Smith, E. R. (2000). Intergroup emotions: Explaining offensive action tendencies in an intergroup context. *Journal of Personality & Social Psychology, 79*(4), (p. 602).

Madlock, P. E. (2008). The link between leadership style, communication competence, and employee satisfaction. *Journal of Business Communication (1973), 45*(1), (pp. 61-78).

Mayer, J. D., & Salovey, P. (1997). What is emotional intelligence? In Salovey, P., & Sluyter, D. (Eds.), *Emotional Development and Emotional Intelligence: Implication for Educators*. New York: Basic Books.

Milgram, S. (1992). *The Individual in a Social World: Essays and Experiments* (2nd ed.). New York: McGraw-Hill.

Nisbett, R. E., Peng, K., Choi, I., & Norenzayan, A. (2001). Culture and systems of thought: Holistic versus analytic cognition. *Psych. Rev. 108*(2), (pp. 291-310).

Noer, D. M. (1993). Leadership in an age of layoffs. *Issues & Observations, 13*(3), (pp. 1-6).

Powell, T. C., Lovallo, D., & Fox, C. (2011). Behavioral strategy. *Strategic Management Journal, 32*(13), (pp. 1369-1386).

Porter, M. (1996). What is strategy? *Harvard Business Review*, November–December, (pp. 61-78).

Roseman, I. J. (1991). Appraisal determinants of discrete emotions. *Cognition and Emotion, 5*(3), (pp. 161-200).

Rosenthal, R., Hall, J. A., DiMatteo, M. R., Rogers, P., Archer, P. D. (1979). Sensitivity to Nonverbal Communication: *A Profile Approach to the Measurement of Individual Differences*. Baltimore: Johns Hopkins University Press.

Rousseau, D. M. (1985). Issues of level in organizational research: Multi-level and cross-level perspectives. *Research in Organizational Behavior, 7*, (pp. 1-37).

Rubin, R. S., Munz, D. C., Bommer, W. H. (2005). Leading from within: The effects of emotion recognition and personality on transformational leadership behavior. *Academy of Management Journal, 48*(5), (pp. 845-858).

Russell, J. A. (2003). Core affect and the psychological construction of emotion. *Psychological Review, 110*(1), (pp. 145-172).

Russell, J. A, & Feldman Barrett, L. (2009). Core affect. In Sander, D. & Scherer, K. R. (Eds.), *The Oxford Companion to Emotion and the Affective Sciences*. Oxford University Press.

Salovey, P., & Mayer, J. D. (1990). Emotional intelligence. *Imagination, Cognition and Personality, 9*(3), (pp. 185-211).

Sanchez-Burks, J. (2005). Protestant relational ideology: The cognitive underpinnings and organizational implications of an American anomaly. *Research in Organizational Behavior, 26*, (pp. 265-305).

Sanchez-Burks, J., & Huy, Q. (2009). Emotional Aperture and Strategic Change: The Accurate Recognition of Collective Emotions. *Organization Science, 20*(1), (pp. 22-34).

Schermerhorn, R. R., Jr., Hunt, J. G., & Osborn, R. N. (2001). *Organizational Behavior* (7th ed.). New York: Wiley.

Smith, C. A., & Ellsworth, P. C. (1985). Patterns of cognitive appraisal in emotion. *Journal of Personality and Social Psychology, 48*(4), (pp. 813-838).

Smith, C. (1989). Dimensions of appraisal and physiological response in emotion. *Journal of Personality and Social Psychology, 56*(3), (pp. 339-353).

Smith, E. R., Seger, C.R., & Mackie, D.A. (2007). Can emotions be truly group level? Evidence regarding four conceptual criteria. *Journal of Personality and Social Psychology, 93*(3), (pp. 431-446).

Stahl, G. K., & Voigt, A. (2008). Do cultural differences matter in mergers and acquisitions? A tentative model and examination. *Organization Science 19*(1), (pp. 160-176).

Staw, B. M., & Barsade, S. G. (1993). Affect and managerial performance: A test of the sadder-but-wiser vs. happier-and-smarter hypotheses. *Administrative Science Quarterly, 38*, (pp. 304-328).

Sy, T., Côté, S., & Saavedra, R. (2005). The contagious leader: impact of the leader's mood on the mood of group members, group affective tone, and group processes. *Journal of Applied Psychology 90*(2), (pp. 295-305).

Tichy, N. M, & Sherman, S. (1994). *Control Your Destiny or Someone Else Will.* New York: Harper Business.

Tiedens, L. Z, & Linton, S. (2001). Judgment under emotional uncertainty: the effects of specific emotions and their associated certainty appraisals on information processing. Working papers (faculty), *Stanford Graduate School of Business*, Stanford University.

To, M. L., Fisher, C. D., Ashkanasy, N. M., & Rowe, P. A. (2012). Within-person relationships between mood and creativity. *Journal of Applied Psychology, 97*(3), (pp. 599-612).

Turner, J. C., Hogg, M. A., Oakes, P. J., Reicher, S. D. & Whetherell, M. S. (1987). *Rediscovering the Social Group: A Self-Categorization Theory.* Oxford, UK & New York, USA: Blackwell.

Vaara, E., Tienari, J., Piekkari, R., & Säntti, R. (2005). Language and the circuits of power in a merging multinational corporation. *Journal of Management Studies, 42*(3), (pp. 595-623).

Van Zomeren, M., Spears, R., & Fischer, A. H. (2004). Put your money where your mouth is! Explaining collective action tendencies through group-based anger and group efficacy. *Journal of Personality and Social Psychology, 87*(5), (pp. 649-664).

Voronov, M., & Vince, R. (2012). Integrating emotions into the analysis of institutional work. *Academy of Management Review, 37*(1), (pp. 58-81).

Weick, K. E., & Quinn, R. E. (1999). Organizational change and development. *Annual Review of Psychology, 50*(1), (p. 361).

Weiss, H. M., & Cropanzano, R. (1996). Affective events theory: A theoretical discussion of the structure, causes and consequences of affective experiences at work. *Research in Organizational Behavior, 18*(1), (pp. 1-74).

Welcomer, S. A., Gioia, D. A., & Kilduff, M. (2000). Resisting the discourse of modernity: Rationality versus emotion in hazardous waste siting. *Human Relations, 53*(9), (pp. 1175-1205).

White, A., Smets, M. & Canwell, A. (2022). Organizational transformation is an emotional journey. Harvard Business Review Online, accessed on July 18. https://hbr.org/2022/07/organizational-transformation-is-an-emotional-journey.

Zeelenberg, M., van Dijk, W. W., Manstead, A., & van der Pligt, J. (2000). On bad decisions and disconfirmed expectancies: The psychology of regret and disappointment. *Cognition and Emotion, 14*(4), (pp. 521-541).

Neuroscience in Strategic Management

Karin Aviva Hirsch, Gerd Nufer, Robin Rüdesheim and Deborah Chaya Simonovich

Abstract. Neuroscience has enriched various social science fields, including anthropology, marketing, law, and political science. Though these disciplines have seen successful integrations with neuroscience, the synergy between brain research and strategic management, termed "neuroscience" by Thomas C. Powell, remains less explored. This article examines the role of neuroscience within strategic management and outlines directions for prospective research.

Keywords: Neuroscience, strategic management, neurostrategy, brain research, decision-making, cognition, functional magnetic resonance imaging (fMRI)

1. Introduction

Strategic management, crucial for an organization's success, offers tools for analyzing, setting, and executing a company's key objectives (Nag et al., 2007). With its focus on long-term decision-making, scholars in strategic management have sought insights from cognitive neuroscience (Hodgkinson, 2008; Cristofaro 2021). This exploration is bolstered by the integration of brain research in fields like anthropology (Adenzato and Garbarini, 2006), law (Chorvat and McCabe, 2004), and political science (Amodio et al., 2007). Such interdisciplinary work has shown the value of merging brain research with social sciences. This article seeks to explore the intersection of strategic management and neuroscience, highlighting challenges and potential avenues for "neurostrategy." It further aims to guide future collaborative efforts between these disciplines.

2. The emergence and development of neuroscience

Neuroscience's beginnings go back to ancient Greece and Rome with historic figures including Hippocrates. By the 19th century, Marie-Jean-Pierre Flourens and other physicians began examining brain function by observing deficits caused by specific brain damage. Various medical investigative techniques, such as magnetoencephalography (MEG), positron emission tomography (PET), galvanic skin response (GSR), electroencephalography (EEG), and functional magnetic resonance imaging (fMRI) (Chen, 2001), help explore neurological mechanisms. Specifically, the non-invasive fMRI has become prominent in cognitive neuroscience due to its ability to track blood oxygenation changes in test subjects while they are engaged in defined tasks (Ogawa et al., 1990).

Today, studies span across cellular, molecular, systemic and behavioral levels. Sub-fields include social, cognitive, and affective neuroscience, with related interdisciplinary themes including neuromarketing and neuroeconomics having implications for strategic management (Nufer, 2020; Bühler et al., 2013).

3. Neurostrategy—limitations and criticism

Rock and Schwartz (2007) believe that understanding recent cognitive science breakthroughs can enhance managerial leadership. However, there is skepticism about melding neuroscience with business strategy. Traditional strategic management often does not delve deeply into individual psychology (Rumelt et al., 1994), which contrasts with neuroscience's focus on individual brain processes (Gul & Posendorfer, 2008). Economists, major contributors to strategic thinking, point out that the findings of brain research are reductionist, and, therefore, question the value of understanding individual decision-making processes for application to broader collective strategic models (Bernheim, 2009).

The decision-makers in multinational firms bring their diverse demographic characteristics of age, gender, nationality, culture, religion, language, education, etc. into their work which impact their neural processes (Laureiro et al., 2015; Cabeza, 2002). However, in contrast to this heterogeneous population in organizations, neuroscience experiments often involve homogeneous samples, questioning the generalizability of these experimental findings. The practicalities of conducting neuroscience experiments, such as using fMRI, are also both costly and time-intensive, leading critics to question their return on investment (Laureiro, 2015).

Interpreting neuroscience data has its challenges. The risk of "reverse interference" can lead to misinterpretation of neural measures, making it hard to associate certain brain signals with specific mental states (Poldrack, 2006). The precise mapping of strategic constructs in the brain might be elusive, diverting resources from potentially more fruitful avenues of study (Dovidio et al., 2008). Bennett and Hacker (2003) caution against confusing brain functions with holistic human experiences, emphasizing the importance of understanding the broader behavioral strategy.

Willingham and Dunn (2003), critically question the real contribution of neuroscience to social science, arguing that recognizing brain regions activated during decisions doesn't necessarily enhance strategic theory. Even if certain patterns are detected in the brain, they might not bring forward new insights for strategic management.

In conclusion, the collaboration between neuroscience and strategic management faces significant skepticism. Critics challenge its generalizability, practical implications, and cost-effectiveness, despite some recognizing its potential merits. The article proceeds to discuss potential collaboration opportunities for neurostrategy research and application.

4. Neurostrategy—potential opportunities for contributions of neuroscience to strategic management

Managers' emotions, cognitions, and social interactions influence company activities and outcomes. Strategy studies have explored beliefs (Denrell, 2008), competitor perceptions (Zajac and Bazerman, 1991), and cognitive frameworks (Prahalad and Bettis, 1986). Three pathways to benefit strategic management from neuroscientific research are discussed below: theory testing, construct validation, and informing strategy practice.

4.1 Theory testing

Neural evidence, such as brain scans, can address unresolved theoretical debates. For instance, the psychological motivations behind sticking to a failing strategy (Staw, 1981) were clarified by Campbell-Meiklejohn et al. (2008), revealing brain activity associated with genuine expectations of positive results.

4.2 Construct validation

Neuroscience can provide physiological evidence for theoretical constructs. For example, the concept of "willingness to pay" is associated with the ventromedial prefrontal cortex activity (Hare et al., 2010). Similarly, "loss aversion" is linked with the ventrolateral prefrontal cortex and striatum (Tom et al., 2007). Such findings support continued hypothesis development.

4.3 Informing strategy practice

Neuroscience applications are evident in the fields of law and politics. Politicians, for instance, use neural studies to appeal to voters' cognitive biases (Westen et al., 2006). Additionally, neuroscience can support strategy implementation through managers' behavioral self-control in their various roles, such as the long-term oriented "planner self" and the short-term compulsive "doer self" (Schelling, 1984). Furthermore, Powell (2011) shows that neural evidence has gained a following in areas such as "affect labeling," "reappraisal," and "mindfulness."

- *Affect labeling:* Individuals jot down their negative feelings, can activate specific brain areas and help regulate emotions, proving more effective in controlling emotional responses than simply discussing or ignoring them (Lieberman et al., 2007; Goldin et al., 2008).

- *Reappraisal:* Managers are placed in a different context for solving problems than in previously accepted methods, such as looking at international market entry from the perspective of the target host country, rather than to familiar home country, and such reappraisal has been shown to activate brain regions associated with complex thinking (Ochsner et al., 2004).

- *Mindfulness:* A cognitive strategy emphasizing open-mindedness regarding alternatives in a strategic context and has been is linked with enhanced well-being and short-term cognition (Levanthal & Rerup, 2006). Mindfulness activates areas associated with emotional regulation and sensory perception, though its long-term effects require more research (Farb et al., 2010; Rock, 2009).

These pathways confirm, neuroscience offers valuable insights for strategic management, indicating a promising interdisciplinary collaboration.

5. Neurostrategy—research gaps and promising collaboration

Blending the disciplines of neuroscience and strategic management could be beneficial, but it is vital to ensure this collaboration would be fruitful. A condensed version of Powell's (2011) perspective on prospective collaborations follows.

Key Considerations for Collaboration:

- Focus on significant issues within the sphere of strategic management.
- Ensure each issue of focus is relevant and intriguing for neuroscientists.
- Any new neural findings in research should enrich understanding among academics and practitioners, whether through theory validation, construct validation, or practical implications.

In addition, three promising avenues for research based on interdisciplinary collaboration, in which the above key considerations would first be applied, have emerged. These fields of interest include reward systems, strategic behavior and leadership, and the agency dilemma, as defined below.

- *Reward Systems*: Both cognitive neuroscience and strategic learning are keen on understanding how reward systems influence habitual behavior (Nelson and Winter, 1982). While bonuses can boost efficiency, they may only be effective for manual tasks. For roles requiring cognitive skills, monetary rewards might even lead to cheating and reduced creativity, transitioning motivation from intrinsic to extrinsic (Fleming, 2011). A shared exploration can elucidate how rewards psychologically impact humans.

- *Strategic Behavior & Leadership*: Visionary entrepreneurs behave differently than seasoned executives of large corporations (Baron, 2007). Certain managers may lack innovative spirit, differing from their more visionary counterparts (Conger and Kanungo, 1987). Merging neuroscience with strategic practices (Rock, 2009) can illuminate which leadership methods and thought processes yield optimal outcomes.

- *The Agency Dilemma*: The conflict of interests between an entity's owners and other stakeholders (principals) and its representatives (agents) is a well-recognized governance issue for organizations, also known as Principal-Agent Theory or Agency Theory. The crux of this issue in strategic management is balancing individual desires while making joint decisions (Blake and Mouton, 1971). Research reveals people advocate more robustly when representing others and constituents prefer assertive representatives, even if it means sidelining other parties or the collective good (Benton and Druckman, 1974; Duck and Fielding,

2003). Integrating these insights with neuroscientific data on the mental states of principals and agents might enhance predictions in experimental and real-world settings.

Despite skepticism, both disciplines exhibit overlapping interests, which could provide platforms for future interdisciplinary research.

6. Conclusion

The integration of neuroscience and strategic management is a relatively novel concept. While neuroscience has been more prominently linked with fields including anthropology, economics, law, politics, and marketing, recent strides have been made to associate it with strategic management, giving birth to the idea of neurostrategy.

Neuroscience predominantly operates on an individual level. Thus, when it merges with strategic management, certain challenges arise. This explains the cautious stance of many strategic management scholars who prefer to observe its implications before fully embracing it. Yet, many factors influencing managerial decisions, such as emotions, cognition, and social perceptions, originate in the brain. Therefore, staying up-to-date on behavioral neuroscience could be beneficial for strategy professionals.

A collaborative approach between strategy researchers and neuroscientists is recommended. By recognizing the potential contributions from both fields, pinpointing collaborative research areas, and establishing lasting relationships, the domain of neurostrategy can thrive. This interdisciplinary alliance can lead to innovative findings that not only serve academia but also have practical implications for society.

References

Adenzato, M., & Garbarini, F. (2006). The as if in cognitive science, neuroscience, and anthropology: a journey among robots, blacksmiths, and neurons. *Theory and Psychology 16*(6), 747–759. doi: 10.1177/0959354306070515

Amodio D. M., & Jost J. T., & Master S. L., & Yee C. M. (2007). Neurocognitive correlates of liberalism and conservatism. *Nature Neuroscience 10*(10), 1246–1247. doi: 10.1038/nn1979

Amodio, D. M. (2006). Stereotyping and evaluation in implicit race prejudice: evidence for independent constructs and unique effects on behavior. *Journal of Personality and Social Psychology, 91*(4), 652-661. doi: 10.1037/0022-3514.91.4.652

Baron, R. A. (2007). Behavioral and cognitive factors in entrepreneurship: entrepreneurs as the active element in new venture communities. *Strategic Entrepreneurship Journal*, *1*(1/2), 167-182. doi: 10.1002/sej.12

Bennett, M. R., & Hacker P. M. S. (2003). *Philosophical Foundations of Neuroscience*. Malden, MA: Blackwell Publishing.

Benton, A. A., & Druckman, D. D (1974). Constituent's bargaining orientation and intergroup negotiations. *Journal of Applied Social Psychology* *4*(2): 141-150.

Bernheim, B. D. (2009). On the potential of neuroeconomics: A critical (but hopeful) appraisal. *American Economic Journal: Microeconomics* *1*(2): 1–41.

Blake, R. R., & Mouton J. S. (1961). Loyalty of representatives to ingroup positions during intergroup competition. *Sociometry* *24*(2): 177–183.

Bühler, A., Häusel, H.-G., & Nufer, G. (2013). Neuromarketing im Sport. In Nufer, G., & Bühler, A. (Eds.), *Marketing im Sport. Grundlagen und Trends des modernen Sportmarketing* (3rd ed.). Berlin: Erich Schmidt Verlag, 417-444.

Cabeza, R. (2002). Hemispheric asymmetry reduction in older adults: the HAROLD model. *Psychology and Aging*, *17*(1), 85.

Campbell-Meiklejohn, M., Woolrich, R., Passingham R., & Rogers R. D. (2008). Knowing when to stop: The brain mechanisms of chasing losses. *Biological Psychiatry*, *63*(3), 29-300. doi: 10.1016/j.biopsych.2007.05.014

Chen, A. (2001). New perspectives in EEG/MEG brain mapping and PET/fMRI neuroimaging of human pain. *International Journal of Psychophysiology*, *42*(2), 147-159.

Chorvat T., & McCabe, K. (2004). The brain and the law. *Philosophical Transactions of the Royal Society, Series B 359*(1451), 1727–1736. doi: 10.1098/rstb.2004.1545

Conger J. A., & Kanungo R. (1987). Toward a behavioral theory of charismatic leadership in organizational settings. *Academy of Management Review*, *12*(4), 637-647. doi: 10.5465/AMR.1987.4306715

Cristofaro M. (2021). Dancing between behavioural strategy and neurostrategy. Towards an affect-cognitive theory of management decision. In: *Emotion, Cognition, and Their Marvellous Interplay in Managerial Decision Making*. Cambridge Scholars Publishing, 239-262.

Dovidio J. F., & Pearson A. R., & Orr P. (2008). Social psychology and neuroscience: Strange bedfellows or a healthy marriage? *Group Processes and Intergroup Relations*, *11*(2), 247–263. doi: 10.1177/1368430207088041

Duck J.M., & Fielding K.S. (2003). Leaders and their treatment of subgroups: Implications for evaluations of the leader and the superordinate group. *European Journal of Social Psychology* *33*(3), 387–401.

Ersner-Hershfield, H., & Wimmer G. E., & Knutson, B. (2009). Saving for the future self: Neural measures of future self-continuity predict temporal discounting. *Social, Cognitive, and Affective Neuroscience*, *4*(1), 85-92. doi: 10.1093/scan/nsn042

Farb, N. A., Anderson, A. K., Mayberg, H., Bean, J., McKeon, D., & Segal, Z.V. (2010). Minding one's emotions: Mindfulness training alters the neural expression of sadness. *Emotion, 10*(1), 25-34. doi: 10.1037/a0017151

Fleming, N. (2011). The bonus myth: How paying for results backfires. *New Scientist, 210*(2807), 40-43.

Golding, P. R., & McRae, K., & Ramel, W., & Gross, J. J. (2008). The neural bases of emotion regulation: Reappraisal and suppression of negative emotion. *Biological Psychiatry, 63*(6), 577-586. doi: 10.1016/j.biopsych.2007.05.031

Gul F., & Pesendorfer W. (2008). The case for mindless economics. In Caplin A., & Schotter A. (Eds)., The Foundations of Positive and Normative Economics: A Handbook. New York: *Oxford University Press*, 3–42.

Hare T. A., Camerer C. F., Knoepfle D. T., O'Dohery, J. P., & Rangel, A. (2010). Value computations in ventral medial prefrontal cortex during charitable decision making incorporate input from regions involved in social cognition. *Journal of Neuroscience, 30*(2), 583-590. doi: 10.1523/JNEUROSCI.4089-09.2010

Hodgkinson, G.P. (2008). Strategic management. In Chmiel N (Ed.), *Introduction to Work and Organizational Psychology: A European Perspective* (2nd ed.). Oxford, U.K.: *Blackwell*, 329–350.

Hsu, M., Krajbich, I., Zhao, C., & Camerer, C. F. (2009). Neural response to reward anticipation under risk is nonlinear in probabilities. *Journal of Neuroscience, 29*(7), 2231-2237. doi: 10.1523/JNEUROSCI.5296-08.2009.

Laureiro, D., Venkatraman, V., Cappa Iuss, S., Zollo, M., & Brusoni, S. (2015). Cognitive Neurosciences and Strategic Management: Challenges and Opportunities in Tying the Knot. *Cognition and Strategy, 32*, 351-370. doi: 10.1016/j.biopsych.2015.04.009

Levinthal, D. A., & Rerup, C. (2006). Crossing an apparent chasm: Bridging mindful and less-mindful perspectives on organizational learning. *Organization Science, 17*(4), 502-513. doi: 10.1287/orsc.1060.0197

Lieberman, M. D., Eisenberger, N. I., Crockett, M. J., Tom, S., Pfeifer, J. H., & Way, B. M. (2007). Putting feelings into words: affect labeling disrupts amygdala activity to affective stimuli. *Psychological Science, 18*(5), 421-428. doi: 10.1111/j.1467-9280.2007.01916.x

Nag, R., Hambrick, D. C., & Chen, M. J. (2007). What is strategic management, really? Inductive derivation of a consensus definition of the field. *Strategic Management Journal 28*(9), 935–955. doi: 10.1002/smj.615

Nelson, R. R., & Winter, S. G. (1982). *An Evolutionary Theory of Economic Change*. Cambridge, MA: Belknap Press.

Nufer, G. (2020). Neuromarketing – Grundlagen, Best-Practice-Beispiele aus dem Handel und kritische Würdigung. *PraxisWissen Marketing – German Journal of Marketing, 5*, 53-68. doi: 10.15459/95451.40

Ochsner, K. N., Ray, R. D., Cooper J.C., Robertson, E. R., Chopra, S., Gabrieli, J. D., & Gross, J. J. (2004). For better or for worse: neural systems supporting the cognitive down- and up- regulation of negative emotion. *Neuroimage, 23*(2), 483-499. doi: 10.1016/j.neuroimage.2004.06.030

Ogawa, S., Lee, T. M., Kay, A. R., & Tank, D. W. (1990). Brain magnetic resonance imaging with contrast dependent on blood oxygenation. *Proceedings of the National Academy of Sciences, 87*(24), 9868-9872.

Phelps E. A. (2009). The study of emotion in neuroeconomics. In Glimcher, P. W., Camerer, C. F., Fehr, E., & Poldrack, R. A. (Eds.), Neuroeconomics: Decision Making and the Brain, New York: *Academic Press,* 233–250.

Poldrack R. A. (2006). Can cognitive processes be inferred from neuroimaging data? *Trends in Cognitive Sciences 10*(2), 59–63. doi: 10.1016/j.tics.2005.12.004

Poldrack, R. A. (2008). The role of fMRI in Cognitive Neuroscience: Where do we stand? *Current Opinion in Neurobiology, 18*(2), 223-227. doi: 10.1016/j.conb.2008.07.006

Powell, T. (2011). Neurostrategy. *Strategic Management Journal, 32*(13), 1484-1499. doi: 10.1002/smj.969

Prahalad, C., & Bettis, R. (1986). The dominant logic: a new linkage between diversity and performance. *Strategic Management Journal, 7*(6), 485-501. doi: 10.1002/smj.4250070602

Rock D., & Schwartz J. (2007): Why neuroscience matters to executives. *Booz & Company.* Retrieved April 10, 2016 from: http://www.strategy-business.com/article/li00021?gko=60b7d.

Rock, D. (2009). *Your Brain at Work.* New York, NY: Harper Collins.

Rumelt R. P., Schendel D., & Teece, D. (Eds.). (1994). *Fundamental Issues in Strategy: A Research Agenda.* Boston, MA: Harvard Business School Press.

Sanfey, A. G., Rilling, J. K., Aronson, J. A., Nystrom, L. E., & Cohen, J. D. (2003). The neural basis of economic decision-making in the ultimatum game. *Science, 300*(5626), 1755-1758. doi: 10.1126/science.1082976

Schelling, T. (1984). Self-command in practice, in policy, and in a theory of rational choice. *The American Economic Review, 74*(2), 1-11.

Staw, B. M. (1975). The escalation of commitment to a course of action. *Academy of Management Review, 6*(4), 577-587. doi: 10.1016/0030-5073(76)90005-2.

Tom, S., Fox, C. R., Trepel, C., & Poldrack, R.A. (2007). The neural basis of loss-aversion in decision-making under risk. *Science, 315*(5811), 515-518. doi: 10.1126/science.1134239

Weber, E. U., & Johnson, E. J. (2009). Mindful judgement and decision making. *Annual Review of Psychology, 60,* 53-85.

Westen, D., Blagov, P., Harenski, K., Kilts, C., & Hamann, S. (2006). Neural bases of motivated reasoning: an fMRI study of emotional constraints on partisan political judgement in the 2004 U.S. presidential election. *Journal of Cognitive Neuroscience, 18*(11), 1947-1958. doi:10.1162/jocn.2006.18.11.1947

Willingham, D. T., & Dunn, E.W. (2003). What neuroimaging and brain localization can do, cannot do, and should not do for social psychology. *Journal of Personality and Social Psychology, 84*(4), 662-671. doi: 10.1037/0022-3514.85.4.662

Wilson, T. D., & Schooler, J. W. (1991). Thinking too much: introspection can reduce the quality of preferences and decisions. *Journal of Personality and Social Psychology, 60*(2), 181-192. doi: 10.1037/0022-3514.60.2.181

Yarkoni, T., & Braver, T. S. (2010). Cognitive neuroscience approaches to individual differences in working memory and executive control: Conceptual and methodological issues. In Gruszka, A., Matthews, G., & Szymura, B. (Eds.), *Handbook of Individual Differences in Cognition: Attention, Memory and Executive Control*, 87-107.

Zajac, E. J., & Bazerman, M. H. (1991). Blind spots in industry and competitor analysis: implications for interfirm (mis)perceptions for strategic decisions. *Academy of Management Review, 16*(1), 37-56. doi: 10.5465/AMR.1991.4278990

Behavioral Game Theory

Robert LoBue, Jonas May, Jörg Naeve and Lukas Schneider

Abstract. This article reviews studies on behavioral game theory, which seeks to enhance traditional game theory by introducing behavioral components. While many game theory studies integrate behavioral aspects of utility, strategic thought, and learning, often via experimental methods, there remain uncharted territories, including the effects of framing or depiction. A limited number of models aim to amalgamate multiple factors for practical, real-world application. Consequently, behavioral game theory has considerable ground to cover before attaining substantial applicability in practice.

Keywords: Behavioral game theory, decision-making, game theory

1. Introduction

Game theory, rooted in mathematical modeling as introduced by von Neumann & Morgenstern in 1944, seeks to depict and scrutinize scenarios involving interactive decision-making (Osborne & Rubinstein, 1994; Gächter, 2004). It employs mathematical models to forecast player actions, hinging on the presumption that players are purely rational, selecting strategies that maximize their benefits. It is believed these players possess a thorough grasp of game dynamics allowing them to anticipate other players' strategies (Camerer, 1997; Gächter, 2004). In a contrasting vein, evolutionary game theory proposes simpler models, suggesting players are unaware they are even in a game, and act on instinctive "programmed strategies" (Weibull, 1997).

Positioned between these polarities is behavioral game theory (BGT). Camerer (1997) contends that the intricate math-driven models can be cumbersome for day-to-day human decision-making. Moreover, evolutionary game theory models do not always align with human decision processes. BGT, therefore, seeks to portray genuine human actions, threading a path between hyper-rational and inadequately rational analyses (Camerer, 1997, p. 167). Still, BGT does not aim to negate traditional models but to refine them, leaning on experimental data for a touch of realism (Gächter, 2004).

Historically, the primary research concern was juxtaposing experimental outcomes with game theoretic equilibrium models, culminating in novel methodologies. Contemporary studies, however, use these behavioral models as experimental benchmarks, evaluating their predictive prowess (Camerer, 2014).

This article's intent is to consolidate literature on BGT, spotlight its research domains, and elucidate pertinent behavioral models. The discussion will also navigate the spectrum of opinions on BGT's current research state and prospective direction. A concluding segment will highlight existing research gaps and provide a forward-looking perspective on BGT.

2. Scholarly contributions to behavioral game theory

Research in behavioral game theory has predominantly revolved around three central themes, as delineated by Camerer, Loewenstein, & Rabin in 2004. First, there is the theme of *social utility*, highlighting players' tendency to factor in not only their own game outcomes but also those of their counterparts. Second, the theme of *strategic reasoning* delves into players' strategy choices, particularly how they align their strategies based on their perceptions of opponents' actions. Third, the theme of *learning* while players interact within the gaming environment is explored. Beyond these primary themes, researchers in the BGT realm have also delved into psychological biases and their influences on *choice and judgement* in decision-making. This realm of themes is explored further in the following sections.

2.1. Social utility

The earliest researchers in game theory, as it originatied in the 1940s, assumed that each player's primary goal would be to maximize their personal gains. However, direct findings of research soon challenged this notion. Notably, studies on the prisoner's dilemma indicated players cooperated more than game theory predicted (Rapoport & Chammah, 1965). This behavior was attributed to social utility, suggesting players consider not just their benefits but also those of others. Real-world experiments, including the trust, ultimatum, and dictator games, continued further to contradict classic game theory.

Fundamentally, in the trust game, as tested with university students as subjects by Berg et al. (1995), a player is given $10 to keep or to forward in part or in whole, i.e. as an investor, to an anonymous trustee. The trustee, when a sum is forwarded, also receives a multiple of the original amount and can keep or return the entire sum in part or in whole. Modern game theory, as developed by John Nash a Princeton professor who earned the Nobel Prize in Mathematics for his pioneering contributions to the field starting from the early 1950s (Nash, 1950; 1953), posits the trustee would not return any gain along with the initial investment, making it also illogical for the investor to offer any sum to the trustee. In the experimental groups tested, a small number of players, investors and trustees, do decide to keep the money to themselves, as was predicted by classical game theorists. Yet, in most variations of the game, $5 or $10 are the sums most often invested, for an average close to $5 overall, and trustees return more than half of the investment, on average. Such cooperative actions, apparently rooted in trust, are termed "positive reciprocity."

Further, in the ultimatum game as first designed and tested by Güth et al. (1982), the experimental results support a social orientation based on the perception of unfairness or fairness. A player is required to split a sum of money with another player. If the second player rejects the offer, neither gets anything. Motivated only by self-interest, it is logical for the second player to accept any offer, no matter how small, from the first player. Furthermore, the first player would be expected to only offer the minimum possible amount required in the experiment to the second player. Yet, experimental data shows consistently that players often decline offers perceived to be unfair, i.e. too small (Thaler, 1988; Rabin, 1993). Players are at times willing to forgo gains in order to punish unfairness, a form of vengeance effect Berg et al. (1995) term "negative reciprocity". Variants of this experiment have also studied cultural influences on the decisions of players of this type of game (Andersen et al., 2011).

Moreover, in the dictator game, a player is provided with a sum of money to keep and is given the option of offering a portion of their amount received to another actor, without the risk of refusal. In variations of the game where the recipients could be other players, charities, or even the experimenters themselves, a portion of the players, at times a minority and others a majority, agree to split the sum with the other actor. This decision has intrigued researchers, with some suggesting it may be not without a motive other than altruism, but rather motivated by social rewards, such as displaying generosity to others (Charness & Rabin, 2002; Engelmann & Strobel, 2006; Berman & Small, 2012; Lazear et al., 2012; Tonin & Vlassopoulos 2013).

Two main models aim to incorporate these empirical findings into game theory (Camerer, 2003). One, the "inequality-aversion" theory, demonstrates how players who value equity, motivated by experimental coefficients which could express feelings of guilt and envy, often sacrifice a purely optimal result to equalize game outcomes (Fehr & Schmidt 1999; Bolton & Ockenfields, 2000). The other focuses on the "theory of reciprocity," positing that players' choices hinge on their perceived intentions of opponents (Rabin, 1993; Falk & Fischbacher, 1998, 2006; Dufwenberg & Kirchsteiger, 2004). Each model has its merits as shown in experiments, and both could contribute to a more comprehensive theoretical model in the future (Camerer, 2003).

In essence, while the assumptions of classic game theory as well as modern game theory have faced challenges, empirical findings on altruism, equity, and both positive and negative reciprocity have enriched the field. Efforts continue to harmonize these findings with foundational game theory principles, but no universally accepted approach has emerged.

2.2. Strategic reasoning

In strategic games, players must anticipate each other's actions and reactions. Classical game theory presents the idea of dominance, where a rational player will always choose the one dominant strategy that is superior to others (Gächter, 2004). However, this methodology becomes ever more complex in dominance-solvable games, where players iteratively reject strategies whose dominance comes into question, often through "backward induction," i.e. reviewing the results of past decisions in playing a game. In addition, evidence also suggests test subjects simply do not always choose to employ dominant strategies (Johnson et al., 2002).

The p-beauty contest game, as explored by Nagel (1995; 1999), is a good example of this complexity. In this game, players select a whole number between 0 and 100, and the winner is the one whose choice is closest to the group's average multiplied by a predetermined and known fraction (p) greater than or equal to 0 but less than 1. Several rounds of the game are played to examine any changes in player strategy. Here, Nash equilibrium logic dictates that with the experience of more iterations, the ideal choice should be zero. For example, where p=0.7, it is fairly simple to observe that 70, 100 times p, is the highest number for all players to logically choose, but thereafter it would also be observed that the upper limit could be 48, 70 times p, and the logical conclusion further is that an infinite series of such multiplications leads to a result nearest to the whole number choice of 0. However, real-world experiments often do not yield this expected result. It appears that players employ "boundedly rational" strategies with limited "depths of reasoning" to evaluate the iterative nature of all of the other players' likely choices.

These observations led to the development of models that attempt to quantify humans' iterative thinking in games (Camerer & Ho, 2014). The level-k Model from Stahl and Wilson (1995) categorizes players based on their mental iteration steps, with "level-0" players apparently not considering the influence of other players' strategies in their choice, leading to a uniform probabilistic range of choices in a game. "Level-1" players first consider that all other players are level-0 types when making their choice in a game. "Level-2" players further assume that their competitors are a mix of level-0 and level-1 players, with their level-1 expectations leading their own final choices (as level-0 results would be expected to be uniform). Therefore, at "level-3", a player considers that level-0 and level-1 players are likely to make up a majority of players, and the expectations of the level-2 competitors will have the greatest influence on the strategic choice. The logic employed by any higher-level player, i.e. "level-k" looking back at "level-k-1" (level k minus 1), would lead back to level-2 as having the greatest strategic influence. Interestingly, the findings from Stahl and Wilson (1995) do identify another type of "worldly" player, who indicates awareness and acceptance of modern game theory choices, e.g. Nash equilibrium behavior, as well as an expectation that competitors are also aware. However, their experiments do not point to another type of player that might be expected, "rational expectations" types who are unboundedly rational players. In related research studies, similar findings are observed. The cognitive hierarchy model presumes that level-k players believe others are level-k-1. Studies also suggest that players typically limit iteration most often to one and two levels (Camerer et al., 2003; Camerer & Ho, 2014).

The models above have been rigorously tested in experimental settings. The cognitive hierarchy and level-k models assume players strategize rationally but might err in predicting others' moves. Conversely, the quantal response equilibrium (QRE) model, introduced by McKelvey & Palfrey (1995), assumes players may err in strategy but still have accurate beliefs about other players' actions. Debates persist over which model is superior in capturing deviations from classical and modern game theory predictions. Some studies find both cognitive hierarchy and QRE models to be similar in performance (Rogers et al., 2009), while others favor the QRE model (Moinas & Pouget, 2013). Camerer (2003) therefore posits that the game type may determine the model's efficacy.

In summary, empirical evidence indicates game players may employ strategic reasoning with limits. The p-beauty contest game, among others, underscores this behavior and has paved the way for two primary models of strategic reasoning. Notably, these models revolve around one-shot games, excluding learning aspects, which are explored further.

2.3. Learning

The models previously discussed aim to clarify how players achieve equilibrium in one-off, dominance-solvable games through iterative thinking. However, these models fall short for recurring games, where equilibrium is achieved via learning during participation, particularly through trial-and-error and the effect of a learning curve. Within the vast realm of learning theories—including traditional rule learning, evolutionary learning, and imitation learning—reinforcement learning and belief learning have been set in the spotlight as particularly relevant to behavioral game theory by many scholars (e.g., Gächter, 2004; Camerer, 2003).

On one hand, reinforcement learning is grounded in the notion that strategies' appeal alters based on past successes. Stemming from the "law of effect," a strategy's previous success dictates its frequency of future use (Camerer, 2003). This idea, originating with pioneers including Bush & Mosteller (1955) and Cross (1973), gained renewed interest in the 1990s and early 2000s as it intersected with decision theory. Camerer (2003), among other researchers, has criticized reinforcement learning as too sluggish for human pacing but has also joined with the theory's proponents as Erev and Roth (1998) demonstrated accurate decision predictions in applications of multi-equilibrium games.

On the other hand, belief learning posits that individuals update their strategies based on their evolving beliefs about other players' actions, using others' past decisions as a guide (Gächter, 2004). This approach shares kinship with "fictitious play" theories, first presented by Brown (1951) and Robinson (1951), where Nash equilibrium was determined through algorithm-based simulations. Although Shapley (1964) originally disproved these theories, later studies discovered test results converge towards equilibrium in about half of the cases (Conitzer, 2009 & Goldberg et al., 2013). Fudenberg & Kreps (1995) also showed that players reasoning regarding past play and competitors' prior choices may be inconsistent or inaccurate in comparison to a pure Nash equilibrium strategy applied in algorithm-based simulations. Jordan (1991) further determined that Nash equilibrium is attained in normal form games where each player knows his or her own payoff function but is unaware of the payoff functions of the other players in the game. Jordan points out that this "Bayesian learning" model could be useful in strategy as competitors' payoffs are normally held as private information.

A hybrid model, the experience-weighted attraction (EWA) learning proposed by Camerer & Ho (1999), bridges reinforcement and belief learning through parameters of psychological interpretation including imagination. This model underscores the idea that all strategic choices, even those that were not chosen, can evolve in appeal post game play. Comparative studies indicate that EWA typically surpasses reinforcement and belief models in performance measuring Nash equilibrium. Although, in mixed-equilibrium games, reinforcement models hold their ground in comparison to EWA. A streamlined version, functional EWA (fEWA), has been developed by Ho et al. (2002), to apply early in more complex experiments as a step which could lead to more advanced EWA models

The journey of understanding learning within games has seen significant advancements in recent times, leading to a plethora of models aiming to explain the effect of learning on strategic choices. Yet, the inherent unpredictability and nuances of learning appear to leave this research field without a consensus on which model or theory should be applied.

2.4. Choice and judgement

Beyond the primary pillars of social utility, strategic reasoning, and learning in behavioral game theory, human decisions are often swayed by psychological biases. These biases diverge from the predictions of traditional game theory. Three of the most noteworthy examples follow, below.

- *Framing Effect*: The manner in which a game or situation is presented to players can influence decision outcomes. A study by Tversky & Kahneman (1992) revealed that individuals are less likely to take risks if the potential outcome of a game is framed as a loss. This "loss aversion" tendency has been observed in various scenarios where disagreement occurs more frequently when bargaining is tied to potential losses (Neale & Bazerman, 1985: Camerer et al., 1993).

- *Overconfidence*: Players sometimes overestimate their capabilities, leading to suboptimal decisions. In a market entry game, where players decide whether to introduce their simulated business model to a market, if all players enter the market, none of them will earn any profits. Therefore, the best decision is for only those whose business models have the highest chances of success to enter the market. However, experiments have shown that players often overestimate their likelihood of success, leading to less-than-ideal choices (Camerer & Lovallo, 1999; Moore 2002).

- *Mental Representation*: Players may struggle, in especially complex games, to form the optimal "decision tree" in their minds, causing their decisions to deviate from logical pathways. This is because rational visualization of decision trees among many available choices can be intellectually challenging as well as mentally taxing (Goldvarg-Steingold & Johnson-Laird, 2002; Devetag & Warglien 2002).

In conclusion, a number of biases and cognitive shortfalls influence human decision-making in games. While this overview covers only the most common examples of existing biases, it underscores that researchers do recognize their existence and impact to game theory. Nonetheless, identifying and understanding these biases in real-world contexts can be especially challenging for researchers in the field of behavioral strategy.

3. Reflection on the state of research

The difference between traditional game theory and behavioral game theory is that the latter aims to take the classical and modern theoretical approaches in order to investigate how humans actually behave and adjust theories accordingly to make them more accurate in predicting behavior, based on controlled experiments with people or algorithm-based simulations. Whereas, the ultimate goal of BGT would be to predict behavior in both experimental and real-world situations (Gächter, 2004). Yet, this would require the development of highly mature models incorporating a wide variety of parameters influencing human decisions. Looking at the literature discussed here, one must note that this field of study still has a long way to go before becoming a practicable method in organizations.

Furthermore, there are contrasting opinions about whether the long-term goal of practicability is realistically achievable or not. Camerer, who is arguably one of the most important representatives of BGT, states that "it appears to be easy to modify theories so self-interested people are humane, and infinite steps become finite, while preserving the central principle in game theory" (2004, p. 466). Conversely, Lucas et al. (2013) defend the research status in the field by recognizing that human decision-making processes naturally incorporate a too complex and thus intangible and inconsistent amount of variable parameters, making it impossible to develop models without biases, heuristics and context dependencies (Lucas et al., 2013).

Reviewing past publications in the field of BGT, it appears that researchers usually focus their work on very specific, isolated parameters as aspects explaining player behavior. Taking into account the findings of the high level of complexity in human decision-making processes, it could be argued, that the current research is largely ignoring the overall picture of BGT. In publications, one can rarely find definitive statements of how the respective work would contribute to the overall goal of predicting human behavior in real life scenarios. However, keeping this overarching objective in mind would be of major importance for this field of study, especially for contributors to avoid getting carried away by discussing marginaly influential issues. One could say that contributions appear to be focusing more and more on peripheral aspects while losing track of the big picture, while a more optimistic view would consider these individual parameters as inputs to a yet undiscovered holistic theory.

4. Research gaps and implications for further research

Research has predominantly aimed to address the recognized limitations of traditional game theory, delving into each suggested parameter individually. Presently, a rich body of empirical data that sets a strong foundation for future exploration is in place. However, for the overarching objective, there remains a need to integrate these previously isolated findings, for example in three stages:

1. *Prioritization of Aspects*: Before combining the elements, it is crucial to determine which are the most essential, as it is improbable that every identified factor can be seamlessly integrated into a singular model.

2. *Broaden Research Scope*: A holistic examination of games can shed light on how certain factors interrelate or stand alone. This broader approach is essential to appreciate the complexity and interconnectedness of game elements.

3. *Creation of an Inclusive Model*: Drawing from the above insights, the final stage would involve crafting a model that marries the

significant behavioral elements, aiming to enhance the predictive capacity of game theory.

For BGT to truly enhance the predictive accuracy of traditional game theory in real-world settings and elevate its practical relevance, it must transcend simple games. The models should be relevant even in complex scenarios. This underscores the need for field research to affirm the validity of BGT in authentic environments. A promising avenue that could offer pertinent insights is the emerging domain of neuro-economics (Fudenberg, 2006; Sanfey, 2007). Two potential areas for further exploration include:

- Implementing BGT in scenarios where groups, rather than individual players, are the competing participants.
- Examining the influence of cultural nuances on behavioral decision-making preferences.

In summary, while there apparently is a long journey ahead before a unified BGT can be fully realized, the current trajectory is promising. We have made significant strides in isolated areas, but the challenge remains in synthesizing these findings and ensuring BGT's practical utility, which is still in its infancy.

5. Conclusion

Empirical research and theoretical modeling have historically attempted to infuse game theory with behavioral elements. However, many of the models discussed remain underdeveloped, often addressing factors in isolation. For a comprehensive model that can predict real-world player decisions, game theory has significant ground to cover. Some skeptics doubt behavioral game theory's potential for real-world applicability, attributing this to its inherent complexity and the unpredictable nature of human psychological factors. On the other hand, some remain hopeful, viewing the existing empirical research as a robust base, poised to birth a refined comprehensive theory in due time.

References

Andersen, S., Ertaç, S., Gneezy, U., Hoffman, M., & List, J. A. (2011). Stakes matter in ultimatum games. *The American Economic Review, 101*(7), 3427-3439.

Arthur, W. B. (1991). Designing economic agents that act like human agents: A behavioral approach to bounded rationality. *The American Economic Review, 81*(2), 353-359.

Arthur, W. B. (1993). On designing economic agents that behave like human agents. *Journal of Evolutionary Economics, 3*(1), 1-22.

Berg, J., Dickhaut, J., & McCabe, K. (1995). Trust, reciprocity, and social history. *Games and Economic Behavior, 10*(1), 122-142.

Berman, J. Z., & Small, D. A. (2012). Self-interest without selfishness: The hedonic benefit of imposed self-interest. *Psychological Science, 23*(10), 1193-1199.

Bolton, G. E., & Ockenfels, A. (2000). ERC: A theory of equity, reciprocity, and competition. *The American Economic Review, 91*(1), 166-193.

Brown, G. W. (1951). Iterative solution of games by fictitious play. *Activity Analysis of Production and Allocation, 13*(1), 374-376.

Bush, R., & Frederick, M. (1995). *Stochastic Models for Learning*. New York: Wiley.

Camerer, C. (1997). Progress in behavioral game theory. *The Journal of Economic Perspectives, 11*(4), 167-188.

Camerer, C. (2003). *Behavioral Game Theory: Experiments in Strategic Interaction*. Princeton University Press.

Camerer, C., & Ho, T. (1999). Experience-weighted attraction learning in normal form games. *Econometrica, 67*(4), 827-874.

Camerer, C., & Ho, T. (2014). Behavioral game theory, experiments and modeling. In Young, H. P., & Zamir, S., Handbook of Game Theory with Economic Applications (Vol. 4, Ch. 10), 517-573.

Camerer, C., Ho, T., & Chong, K. (2002). Sophisticated experience-weighted attraction learning and strategic teaching in repeated games. *Journal of Economic Theory, 104*(1), 137-188.

Camerer, C., Ho, T., & Chong, K. (2003). Models of thinking, learning, and teaching in games. *The American Economic Review, 93*(2), 192-195.

Camerer, C., Johnson, E., Rymon, T., & Sen, S. (1993). Cognition and framing in sequential bargaining for gains and losses. *Frontiers of Game Theory, 104*, 27-47.

Camerer, C., Loewenstein, G., & Rabin, M. (Eds.) (2004). *Advances in Behavioral Economics*. Princeton University Press.

Camerer, C., & Lovallo, D. (1999). Overconfidence and excess entry: An experimental approach. *The American Economic Review, 89*(1), 306-318.

Charness, G., & Rabin, M. (2002). Understanding social preferences with simple tests. *Quarterly Journal of Economics, 117*(3), 817-869.

Conitzer, V. (2009). Approximation guarantees for fictitious play. In *2009 47th Annual Allerton Conference on Communication, Control, and Computing (Allerton)*, September, IEEE, 636-643.

Costa-Gomes, M., Crawford, V. P., & Broseta, B. (2001). Cognition and behavior in normal-form games: An experimental study. *Econometrica, 69*(5), 1193-1235.

Cross, J. G. (1973). A stochastic learning model of economic behavior. *The Quarterly Journal of Economics, 87*(2), 239-266.

Devetag, G., & Warglien, M. (2002). Representing others' preferences in mixed motive games: Was Schelling right? *University of Trento Cognitive Science Laboratory*. Available at SSRN 708103.

Dufwenberg, M., & Kirchsteiger, G. (2004). A theory of sequential reciprocity. *Games and Economic Behavior, 47*(2), 268-298.

Engelmann, D., & Strobel, M. (2006). Inequality aversion, efficiency, and maximin preferences in simple distribution experiments: Reply. *The American Economic Review, 96*(5), 1918-1923.

Erev, I., & Roth, A. E. (1998). Predicting how people play games: Reinforcement learning in experimental games with unique, mixed strategy equilibria. *The American Economic Review, 88*(4), 848-881.

Falk, A., & Fischbacher, U. (2006). A theory of reciprocity. *Games and Economic Behavior, 54*(2), 293-315.

Fehr, E., & Schmidt, K. M. (1999). A theory of fairness, competition, and cooperation. *Quarterly Journal of Economics, 114*(3), 817-868.

Fudenberg, D. (2006). Advancing beyond advances in behavioral economics. *Journal of Economic Literature, 44*(3), 694-711.

Fudenberg, D., & Kreps, D. M. (1994). Learning in extensive-form games I. Self-confirming equilibria. *Games and Economic Behavior, 8*(1), 20-55.

Gächter, S. (2004). Behavioral game theory. In Koehler, D. J., & Harvey, N. (Eds.), *Blackwell Handbook of Judgment and Decision Making*. Malden, MA USA: Blackwell Publishing, 485-503.

Goldberg, P. W., Savani, R., Sørensen, T. B., & Ventre, C. (2013). On the approximation performance of fictitious play in finite games. *International Journal of Game Theory, 42*(4), 1059-1083.

Goldvarg-Steingold, E., & Johnson-Laird, N. P. (2002). Naïve strategic thinking and the representation of games. *Working paper, Princeton University*.

Güth, W., Schmittberger, R., & Schwarze, B. (1982). An experimental analysis of ultimatum bargaining. *Journal of Economic Behavior & Organization, 3*(4), 367-388.

Holt, C. A., & Goeree, J. K. (1999). Stochastic game theory: For playing games, not just for doing theory (No. 306). *University of Virginia, Department of Economics*.

Johnson, E. J., Camerer, C., Sen, S., & Rymon, T. (2002). Detecting failures of backward induction: Monitoring information search in sequential bargaining. *Journal of Economic Theory, 104*(1), 16-47.

Jordan, J. S. (1991). Bayesian learning in normal form games. *Games and Economic Behavior, 3*(1), 60-81.

Kahneman, D., Knetsch, J. L., & Thaler, R. (1986). Fairness as a constraint on profit seeking: Entitlements in the market. *The American Economic Review, 76*(4), 728-741.

Lazear, E P., Malmendier, U., & Weber, R. A. (2012). Sorting in experiments with application to social preferences. *American Economic Journal: Applied Economics, 4*(1), 136-163.

Lucas, G. M., McCubbins, M. D., & Turner, M. B. (2013). Can we build behavioral game theory? Available at SSRN 2278029.

McAllister, P. H. (1991). Adaptive approaches to stochastic programming. *Annals of Operations Research, 30*(1), 45-62.

McKelvey, R. D., & Palfrey, T. R. (1995). Quantal response equilibria for normal form games. *Games and Economic Behavior, 10*(1), 6-38.

Moinas, S., & Pouget, S. (2013). The bubble game: an experimental study of speculation. *Econometrica, 81*(4), 1507-1539.

Mookherjee, D., & Sopher, B. (1994). Learning behavior in an experimental matching pennies game. *Games and Economic Behavior, 7*(1), 62-91.

Mookherjee, D., & Sopher, B. (1997). Learning and decision costs in experimental constant sum games. *Games and Economic Behavior, 19*(1), 97-132.

Moore, D. (2002). Strategic foresight in market entry decisions: An experimental approach. *Working paper, Carnegie-Mellon University.*

Nagel, R. (1995). Unraveling in guessing games: An experimental study. *The American Economic Review, 85*(5), 1313-1326.

Nagel, R. (1999). A survey on experimental beauty contest games: Bounded rationality and learning. In Budescu, D. V., Erev, I., & Zwick (Eds.), *Games and Human Behavior: Essays in Honor of Amnon Rapoport*, Lawrence Erlbaum Associates Publishers, 105-142.

Nash, J. F. (1950). The bargaining problem. *Econometrica, 18*(2), 155-162.

Nash, J. F. (1953). Two person cooperative games. *Econometrica, 21*(1), 128-140.

Neale, M. A., & Bazerman, M. H. (1985). The effects of framing and negotiator overconfidence on bargaining behaviors and outcomes. *Academy of Management Journal, 28*(1), 34-49.

Oosterbeek, H., Sloof, R., & Van De Kuilen, G. (2004). Cultural differences in ultimatum game experiments: Evidence from a meta-analysis. *Experimental Economics, 7*(2), 171-188.

Osborne, M. J., & Rubinstein, A. (1994). *A Course in Game Theory.* Cambridge, MA: The MIT Press.

Rabin, M. (1993). Incorporating fairness into game theory and economics. *The American Economic Review, 83*(5), 1281-1302.

Rapoport, A., & Chammah, A. M. (1965). *Prisoner's Dilemma: A Study in Conflict and Cooperation.* Ann Arbor, MI: University of Michigan Press.

Robinson, J. (1951) An iterative method of solving a game. *Annals of Mathematics, 54*(2), 296-301.

Roth, A. E., & Erev, I. (1995). Learning in extensive-form games: Experimental data and simple dynamic models in the intermediate term. *Games and Economic Behavior, 8*(1), 164-212.

Sanfey, A. G. (2007). Social decision-making: insights from game theory and neuroscience. *Science, 318*(5850), 598-602.

Shapley, L. S. (1964) Some topics in two-person games. *Advances in Game Theory, 52,* 1-2.

Stahl, D. O., & Wilson, P. W. (1995). On players' models of other players: Theory and experimental evidence. *Games and Economic Behavior, 10*(1), 218-254.

Tonin, M., & Vlassopoulos, M. (2013). Experimental evidence of self-image concerns as motivation for giving. *Journal of Economic Behavior & Organization, 90,* 19-27.

Thaler, R. H., (1988). Anomolies: The ultimate game. *Journal of Economic Perspectives, 2*(4), Fall, 195-207.

Tversky, A., & Kahneman, D. (1992). Advances in prospect theory: Cumulative representation of uncertainty. *Journal of Risk and Uncertainty, 5*(4), 297-323.

Vahid, F., & Sarin, R. (2001). Strategy similarity and coordination (No. 8/01). *Monash University, Department of Econometrics and Business Statistics.*

Von Neumann, J., & Morgenstern, O (1947), *Games and Economic Behavior* (2nd rev. ed.). Princeton University Press.

Weibull, J. W. (1997). *Evolutionary Game Theory.* Cambridge, MA: The MIT Press.

Wright, J. R., & Leyton-Brown, K. (2012). Evaluating, understanding, and improving behavioral game theory models for predicting human behavior in unrepeated normal-form games. Available at researchgate.net: arXiv:1306.0918.